Limitless

Elevate Your Existence, Manifest Your Dreams

Mart Tweedy

Limitless
Elevate Your Existence, Manifest Your Dreams
© 2024 Mart Tweedy

ISBN: 9781068562303 Paperback

Published by: Inspired By Publishing

The strategies in this book are presented primarily for enjoyment and educational purposes. Every effort has been made to trace copyright holders and obtain their permission for the use of copyright material.

The information and resources provided in this book are based upon the authors' personal experiences. Any outcome, income statements or other results, are based on the authors' experiences and there is no guarantee that your experience will be the same. There is an inherent risk in any business enterprise or activity and there is no guarantee that you will have similar results as the author as a result of reading this book.

The author reserves the right to make changes and assumes no responsibility or liability whatsoever on behalf of any purchaser or reader of these materials.

Dedication

This book is dedicated to my granda, Ken Dobson, who led me down this road of self-discovery, and to my beautiful boy, Jakey, who brightens my existence and gives me purpose and reason for all that I do.

Jakey, may this book be your light to fight the shadows.

Acknowledgements

I'm deeply grateful to acknowledge the many wonderful people who have supported and contributed to the creation of this book. Each of you has played an indispensable role in bringing these pages to life, and for that, I'm eternally thankful.

First and foremost, to my little one, Jakey, who arrived in the midst of writing this book. You've infused every word with joy and wonder, thank you for reminding me of the magic we all hold within.

To my partner, Jonny, for always encouraging me and enabling me to be my truest self.

To my mam, who helped out on so many occasions with babysitting, cleaning and office work, thank you for all your help and allowing me the time to actually write this book.

To the rest of my dear friends and family who have provided endless encouragement and understanding, thank you for standing by me when my focus needed to be on this. Your support and love mean the world to me.

I would also like to thank my friend, Fran – your guidance over the last three years has been invaluable in writing this book. What I've learned from you as a strong, independent, single mother and business bestie has shaped my life for the better and taken me from the darkest depths to where I am today.

A special thanks goes to my publisher, Chloë, whose keen insights and patient guidance helped shape this manuscript into something I'm proud to share with the world. Your expertise and dedication to this project have not gone unnoticed, and I'm truly grateful for your contributions.

A profound acknowledgement goes to the vibrant community of readers and fellow writers whose stories and insights have inspired and motivated me over the last few years. This book is also yours, in many ways.

And finally, to JJ, our faithful dog, thank you for the countless walks that helped clear my mind and the companionship that comforted me during long nights of writing.

Thank you all for being part of this incredible journey. This book is a testament to the power of collaboration, love and the relentless pursuit of passion.

Here's to more adventures together in the pages yet unwritten.

Foreword

I'm absolutely thrilled to introduce you to a book that I truly believe has the potential to transform not just your daily routines, but your entire outlook on life.

Having connected with Mart in the most serendipitous of ways over the last three years, I've been privileged to watch this gem of a manuscript take shape, blossoming from our shared conversations about life's deepest questions into the powerful guide you now hold in your hands.

You're about to embark on a journey – an exploration into the realms of mindfulness, spirituality and personal growth.

In our busy lives, it's all too easy to forget the importance of pausing, of breathing deeply and of truly living in the moment. This book offers you an oasis, a peaceful space where you can slow down and reconnect with the core of your being.

I fondly recall the many discussions Mart and I shared about the magic hidden in everyday moments and how transformative it can be to simply pay attention.

These conversations are woven into the pages of this book, which invites you to discover the beauty and power in the ordinary, turning routine into something sacred.

Through thoughtful insights, practical advice and engaging personal stories, this book doesn't just present theories – it brings them to life. You'll be immersed in a narrative that not only teaches, but also touches the heart, encouraging you to apply these lessons in ways that are both meaningful and impactful.

Whether it's learning to appreciate the calming ritual of morning tea or understanding the impact of quiet reflection, each chapter offers golden nuggets of wisdom waiting to be unearthed.

As someone who has personally applied these teachings in my own life and manifested some incredible opportunities, I can attest to their transformative power. The practices detailed in this book have enriched my daily life, making each day brighter and more intentional. They've taught me that spirituality isn't about escaping life but about diving deeper into it, embracing every moment with enthusiasm and joy.

Now, I pass this treasure on to you.

As you delve into this book, I encourage you to do so with an open heart and a spirit of adventure. Engage with the exercises, embrace the rituals and don't be afraid to let these new practices challenge and change you. This book is so much more than a guide – it's a companion on your journey towards a richer, more connected life.

As you read on and head out on this adventure, embrace the lessons waiting to unfold and the joy of discovering the profound power within these pages – and within yourself – to craft a life filled with joy, harmony and deep satisfaction.

It's time to live your most magical life, filled with wonder and limitless possibilities.

Francesca Amber

Podcast Host of *Law of Attraction Changed My Life*

Contents

Introduction

I'm not here to prove anything or to tell you that my way of thinking is the ultimate truth.

I'm here to share a perspective that has truly changed my life.

This perspective – which is what I'm about to share in this book – has taken me from being a guy in his 30s with big dreams and in £30,000 of debt, to creating a life that's greater than I ever imagined. The things I've made happen and the stories I'll tell you in this book will blow your mind.

This journey has taught me one compelling truth: Nothing is set in stone. In fact, one of the biggest myths we live by is thinking that the world around us is static and unchanging.

We often believe we're just physical beings in a physical world, made of solid stuff.

We think our experiences as children, shaped by both nature and nurture, decide who we become as adults. As grown-ups, we assign ourselves labels like "I'm anxious," "I'm depressed," or "I'm divorced," and these become the stories we tell ourselves about who we are.

But here's the thing: We're not solid beings in a solid world. Quantum physics has shown us that what we think of as solid matter is actually made up of energy and vibrations.

At the most basic level, everything is made of energy, and our thoughts and beliefs shape this energy into the reality we experience.

When I was stuck in debt and feeling hopeless, I started to realise that my thoughts and beliefs were helping to create my reality. I figured out that by changing my mindset, I could change my life.

The first thing I did was to change how I saw myself.

I began to practise visualisation, positive affirmations and other techniques to align my energy with the life I wanted to create.

I stopped thinking of myself as a victim of circumstance and started seeing myself as a powerful creator. I let go of limiting beliefs and negative labels. I began to see myself as successful, prosperous and capable. This shift in how I thought about myself triggered amazing changes in my life. Once I embraced this new way of thinking, opportunities started appearing almost magically. I met mentors who guided me, found resources that helped me pay off my debt and discovered passions that turned into profitable ventures.

My life changed in ways I couldn't have dreamed of before.

The stories and experiences I share in this book aren't just about making money or gaining material things. They're about the profound change that happens when we understand our true nature as beings of energy. When we tap into this understanding, we unlock the potential to create a life that truly resonates with our deepest desires.

The journey I'm inviting you on is one of self-discovery and empowerment. It's about realising that you're not defined by your past or the labels you've been given. You are a dynamic, ever-changing being with the power to shape your reality. By embracing this truth, you can start to create the life you've always dreamed about.

Think about it: How often do we let labels and past experiences dictate our future? We say things like, "I'm not good at that," or "I've never been lucky," and these statements become self-fulfilling prophecies.

Instead, what if we realised we're capable of growth and change? What if we decided to rewrite our stories, focusing on what we can achieve rather than what holds us back?

As you read through these pages, keep an open mind. Allow yourself to explore the possibilities that come when you let go of old beliefs and embrace the idea that you are a powerful creator.

The world isn't as solid as it seems, and neither are you. Imagine a life where you wake up every day excited about what's to come, where you feel empowered to pursue your dreams and confident in your ability to achieve them. This can be your reality. By understanding the true nature of our world and changing the way you think, you can manifest a life that truly fulfils you.

Take a moment now to reflect on your life.

What stories have you been telling yourself?

What labels have you accepted that might be holding you back?

As you read this book, I encourage you to challenge those beliefs. Open yourself up to new possibilities and start to see yourself as the creative being you truly are.

I urge you to actively engage with this material and apply the techniques in your day-to-day life. To further enrich your experience, make sure to explore the online resources area mentioned throughout the book at cannycrystalsacademy. co.uk/limitless.

There, you'll find additional tools, exercises and content designed to complement the strategies discussed in these pages and enhance your learning. This interactive component is crucial for taking real steps toward personal growth and empowerment, providing you with a practical way to implement the lessons in this book and see tangible results.

The journey ahead is one of transformation and discovery. It's about unlocking your potential and realising that you have the power to create a life beyond your wildest dreams.

I'm excited to share this journey with you and to see what amazing things you'll go on to create.

Chapter 1
My Spiritual Awakening

Imagine walking through life with a veil over your eyes, seeing only the outlines of greater possibilities, never fully grasping the vivid colours of immense potential around you. This chapter isn't just my story; it's a mirror reflecting a journey of transformation that awaits anyone brave enough to step into the realm of spirituality.

What if you continued to walk past this mirror, never stopping to peer into its depths?

Consider the alignment with your true self that could pass by unnoticed. By ignoring this call to deeper understanding, you risk living a shadow of the life that could be, never fully engaging with the deepest, most vibrant experiences that shape our fullest existence.

Most people have a spiritual awakening following either a traumatic experience or feeling totally lost in life; I'm no exception.

As far back as I can remember, I've always had an interest in tarot cards and psychic mediums. I've visited numerous spiritualist churches and been generally obsessed with anything supernatural. My favourite TV shows growing up were fantasy shows such as *Buffy the Vampire Slayer* and *Charmed.* When I saw these people on TV calling themselves "witches," I somehow connected with them – whether it was partly because I, too, felt like an outcast due to my then-hidden homosexuality, or because I believed that maybe there was more to life than just the black-and-white images we're fed by mainstream media as we grow up.

Growing up, my family had very little. Don't get me wrong, we always had the essentials like food, water, electricity, and heating, but my family was far from well-off. My parents separated before I turned one, and my grandparents – my "nanna" and "granda" – helped raise me whilst my mother, whom I called "mam," went out to earn money. It wasn't long before I started to call my nanna "mam," and my mam eventually sacrificed her job to raise me.

Times were tough. I have vague memories of grabbing toy catalogues on the run-up to Christmas and writing down expensive things that I wanted Santa Claus to bring me, oblivious to the fact that it would be my mam and her hard-earned cash purchasing them for me. She did the best she could in a bad situation.

We never had an abundance of anything in our family – except for love.

We were such a close-knit family and still are to this day. As I didn't have a genuine relationship with my dad, my granda was the main father figure in my life. He would give me advice, show me how to do things and was always there for me when I needed a shoulder to cry on or even just a chat about how my day went. My grandparents lived a five-minute walk from me, and I would visit them almost daily.

I grew up in a small mining village in County Durham where most people were Caucasian, British and living in poverty. To put this into context, there was only one person of colour in my year at school, and he stuck out like a sore thumb. For that reason, I tried my hardest to fit into societal norms and avoid drawing attention to my interest in spirituality – let alone the fact that I knew I was gay.

Some of my earliest memories include having a paper bag thrown at me on a school trip containing an apple, a soggy tuna sandwich and a mushed-up bourbon biscuit – their version of a "free school packed lunch." Another time, I remember my mam sending me to school in a bobble-knit burgundy jumper, and our headteacher muttered, "Can't your mother afford the uniform?" as she elbowed me out of the school year photograph for not wearing the correct attire. I found it hard to be myself, and there were several occasions when I thought, "There has to be more to life than this..."

For many years of my life, I struggled with everything. Money was hard to come by, and I always felt that it was in one hand and straight back out the other. I left school, and all the friends I had went to university.

As I'd learned over the years that university was going to be expensive, I assumed I couldn't afford to attend and expected my mam would have to cover the costs. With that in mind, I made the selfless decision to go straight into an apprenticeship, not realising that university fees could be repaid once I was earning over a certain amount. After the apprenticeship, I hopped from job to job with no real vision for where I was headed in life, and I never felt as though I had any true purpose for living.

I'd watch my mam work every hour she could and still struggle financially. Was I just supposed to do the same until I retired?

I secured a job in the National Health Service (NHS) in 2007 and started earning a decent wage working in A&E. However, the job quickly took its toll, and I moved through about 10 different roles over the coming years, steadily climbing the ladder and getting a better wage with each promotion. Like most of the UK, I was travelling to work at 7:30am, getting home at 5:30pm, and visiting friends and family in the little spare time I had. I racked up debt month after month trying to live the same lifestyle as my friends, going out drinking several times a week – "keeping up with the Joneses," if you like!

In 2016, I vividly remember seeing someone on Facebook post about a book called *The Secret*. I honestly had no idea what it was about.

Looking back, I Googled it thinking it was a novel! For those who don't know, it's a book about manifesting desires through positive thoughts and intentions.

After suppressing my spiritual side for so many years, I read the blurb online and got excited for it to arrive.

Manifestation was a new concept to me, so when the book arrived and I realised it was pretty "woo-woo" and spiritual, I was hooked.

Using the techniques described in the book, I started visualising my desired daily life. I would use whatever free time I had to close my eyes and picture myself in different scenarios, feeling all the associated feelings and emotions that would come up because of it.

I slowly started telling friends about this, though I still had that lingering fear and limiting belief that they'd think I was "odd" or "weird" for even believing in such a concept.

To test if my visualisations were working, I decided to manifest something tangible, something I could measure.

It was a cold December evening, and I ran myself a bath to warm through. Whilst having a soak, I decided to set myself a goal of manifesting £3,500 for a three-week holiday to Thailand.

At the time, I had about £15,000 worth of debt and was basically working every hour just to survive – pretty much like the rest of the country – so I hadn't had a holiday in a good few years.

So there I was each evening in the bath, using that time to visualise myself on beaches, feeling the warmth of the sun on my skin. I played the sounds of waves crashing on my phone to emulate actually being there – going on excursions, feeding elephants, having nice Thai meals with my partner and seeing the sights – all whilst visualising that £3,500 surplus in my bank account and what it could afford me.

One day, shortly after visualising during meditation, I remember seeing an advert online for a new series of a TV game show called *Tipping Point*.

The ad was calling for contestants, and I thought, "What's the harm?"

Within ten minutes, I took inspired action, filled out the online application and submitted it.

About a month later, I was invited to a little audition at a hotel in my now-hometown of Newcastle. I was petrified attending the audition and when I'm nervous, I tend to word-vomit. I was now in a room with 30 people, all wanting to be on the show. I was asked to sit in front of them all, look down a camera lens and talk about myself for two minutes. I kept the faith in the back of my mind that this was all part of the process, one step closer to achieving my goal.

I must have done something right, as after a few more weeks passed, I received a call asking if I would like to be a contestant on the show. The producers loved my audition, and I was now being invited to go on national TV!

I couldn't believe it. Things like this had never happened to me before, and I started to think that this might be my big break in life, allowing me to finally get ahead of the game and win some money. I felt – and more importantly, *believed* – that everything was lining up and conspiring in my favour.

I remember taking *The Secret* with me to read on the train ride down to the studios in Bristol, and listening to the audiobook version on my headphones, too. I always felt that, due to my short attention span, I took in information easier if I was reading along at the same time as having it spoken to me.

Even in my hotel room the night before, I was practising the techniques spoken about in the book and visualising what it would be like to win that money, allowing both myself and my partner to head off on holiday.

It'll be no surprise to you, that out of the four contestants on the game show for that day, I ended up being the winner!

And the amount I won?

£3,500!

Do you know that feeling when you get those moments in life that really make the hairs on your arms stand on end? This was definitely one of those times. Had I really manifested £3,500?! It didn't seem like it took too much effort. Could I do it again? Could I manifest more next time? Could I manifest a new car? What about £50,000?

All these thoughts and questions were racing through my mind, and as I rang home to let my family know about my win, I decided to keep the manifestation detail to myself, fearing my family would think I'd lost the plot!

The only person I confided in about my entire experience was my partner, Jonny, and even he gave me a funny look as he nodded and smiled back at me.

The more I told friends about what had happened, the more I got shot down with weird looks and the impression that they thought I'd officially cracked up. Manifestation is a hard concept to explain to closed-minded non-believers, isn't it?

I remember asking Jonny to read *The Secret* one day, leaving the book on his bedside table. A few days later, he came to me and said, "You'll never guess what? I visualised something small, a £50 note...and today my boss gave me two £50 notes to say thank you for going above and beyond!" I'll never forget the look of pure shock and delight on his face. I finally had someone close to me who believed in what I experienced.

That is what solidified it for me. I was thinking, "OK, this definitely works – I've cracked it!" I confided in my mam and tried to drip-feed the concept to her through a conversation about what had happened to me. In response, she told me that I needed to get my head out of "cloud cuckoo land." A part of me believed her at that moment, but a bigger part of me knew that I'd manifested this win and it was because of my visualising, taking action and keeping the faith.

Although I knew I was more than capable of creating my own reality, the self-doubt crept back in. The thoughts of, "I'm 30 years old now, time to buckle up at work and put my head down if I want to climb the ladder," flooded my mind. I couldn't just rely on a concept to get me where I wanted to be in life...

...could I?

So, guess what happened for the next three years? Maybe I manifested the house of my dreams? Manifested myself a family? Manifested a million pounds in my bank account?

No, actually. Absolutely nothing happened!

What happened was I got in my own way. I'd proven to myself that manifesting worked; I knew it did. But life was busy and I just didn't take any time for myself.

Flash forward to 2019. At that point, I'd been working in the NHS for 12 years and was *still* in debt. I had credit cards, was struggling to get a mortgage; I survived day-to-day, but money was so tight. How could I be in a £30,000 a year job but still struggle to make ends meet? I started meditating and visualising again, in the hope that I could somehow manifest myself a better-paying job.

I've always had a keen interest in social media and always had the belief that one day I'd make it and I'd be on TV again. So, I started visualising myself sitting on the *This Morning* couch with Alison Hammond, chatting away and being interviewed. What's funny is, Alison wasn't even one of the main presenters of the show at this point. She would do links for competitions and they would send her to different countries to report. Yet, I could hear her infectious laughter in my head. I could see the camera crew running around behind the scenes. I could see myself sitting in the Green Room with her. I was living those thoughts as though they were gospel.

One day, my then-friend Amber Gill approached me and told me she was in line to be on a TV show called *Love Island* that would be running for eight weeks. She asked if I would look after all her social media channels whilst she was on the show. Obviously, I jumped at the opportunity, and a few weeks later, after she was flown out, things started to get crazy.

From overseeing Amber's social media, I got invited to be interviewed on *BBC Radio 1* and *BBC News Breakfast*, and I was on *Capital* and the local radio almost daily. The *Huffington Post* even ran an article on me, branding my work "the most successful reality TV social media campaign of all time"!

And then came the manifestation result: I got an invitation by email to be interviewed on *This Morning*. At that moment, I knew deep down inside that this was because I'd visualised the interview a couple of months prior. I remember speaking to one of the show's producers on the phone, and just like in my visualisation, I asked if Alison was going to be around. But alas, I was told "no."

On the day, I was taken to the TV studio in London. I was well looked after by all the staff backstage – treated like absolute royalty, in fact.

About an hour had passed, and, as if by magic, I heard a cackle outside of the Green Room.

I knew who that laughter belonged to.

Guess who came in on her day off?

Alison. Hammond.

Honestly, I can't even describe how I felt at that moment. It was exactly how I had envisioned – just like when I won the £3,500 – and it jolted me back into the realisation that visualisation and manifestation really worked!

Flash forward to the 29th of July 2019. There I was, on top of the world: It was the *Love Island* finale and Amber was in the running to win. Our mortgage had gone through that same morning, after six months of back and forth. We got the keys for our brand-new house at 5pm, and by 7pm we were out at a *Love Island* finale party. Amber won the whole show. Obviously, I was ecstatic – hysterical, in fact.

I remember being pulled up on stage in front of everyone at the viewing party, and I was sobbing. It was a triumphant moment for me because I'd run the whole social media campaign on the outside, and I really felt as though I played a part in my friend winning the show. After the party, we got home a bit later than planned and, still on cloud nine, I headed to bed.

The next morning, I was lying in bed asleep when my phone started ringing. I assumed it was a journalist that had got my number and wanted a chat, or a radio station that wanted to talk to me about Amber's win.

It was my mam calling.

My gut sank, and as I sat upright, I knew that something was wrong. It was 6am. She would never ring at such a time. In a blind panic, I answered.

I relive that call over and over in my head.

My mam's voice was shaking as she told me that whilst I was out celebrating the night before, my granda had been taken to hospital for intense pain that came on instantly.

She told me that nobody in the family had wanted to call and spoil my night, but unfortunately, my granda had passed away.

I'd only spoken to him the day before – how could he have died? He wasn't ill. Apparently, his pain came on so suddenly, and he passed away in the ambulance en route to the hospital.

As I mentioned earlier, my granda raised me. I didn't have a relationship with my dad growing up, so my granda was the father figure in my life. I jumped out of bed in tears. I vaguely remember getting in the shower and sobbing like a baby as I stood under the running water. I could barely function. I can't remember getting dressed or driving over to see my family in Durham, but I know I did.

In an instant, I felt like my entire world had fallen apart.

The next few months were a blur to me. I closed myself off from friends and family. I would only leave the house to go to work. I would lay in the bath for hours on end, and, slowly but surely, could feel myself starting to spiral.

I was unable to see past my grief. A few of my friends had taken their own lives that year, too, and I was starting to question everything. I thought, "Is this where I'm headed as well?"

"Am I clinically depressed?"

"Will this pain last forever?"

"Is this the end for me?"

I knew I was a strong-willed person, but this grief was breaking me, and the heartache was just too much for me to live with.

One day, I remember quite vividly calling out to the Universe whilst out on a dog walk, crying into my jacket collar. I asked for a sign that things were going to get better, because I was quite literally on the brink of ending it all. I just wanted a signal that what people were telling me was true, that things *do* get better in time.

I did the same thing that evening. I ran myself a bath, and as I sat there in silence in a zombie-like trance, I looked up and shouted, "Show me things will get better!"

A few days after my outburst, I received notification that the NHS were sending me to Liverpool on a work-trip to visit other trusts. I accepted, hoping that the time away would take my mind off things and allow me a little space on my own.

When I arrived in Liverpool, I booked myself a hire car, and the girl who served me in the office, Carly, recognised me from TV. We immediately got on like a house on fire, realising we had quite a lot in common. We ended up following each other on Instagram.

A few months later, Carly opened up a crystal shop online. Since she had been so nice to me when I was in Liverpool, I supported her and bought a box of five tumblestone crystals, not having a clue what they were about. I vaguely remembered that Amber had been quite into crystals herself. I wondered, had she won *Love Island* with help from her crystals?"

Carly had specifically recommended crystals for dissipating grief and enhancing purpose in life. When they arrived a few days later, I did a little research online and started carrying them around with me daily.

Each time the sun shone on my garden, I would take out my mirror plate and place my crystals on it, ensuring they were being cleansed and charged. I would take them back inside each evening, pop them on my bedside table and vocally ask them to transform my mindset on life.

Steadily, grieving got a little easier, doors started opening for me and my mental health seemed to improve day by day. The more it did, the more crystals I ended up buying.

Over the next 18 months, I somehow accumulated over 200 crystals of my own, each with its own unique and magical healing properties.

At this point in my story, it's now 2020 and we're in the depths of the Coronavirus pandemic. Jonny and I were both working from home, and I was constantly coming up with various ways to take advantage of all the free time we had on evenings and weekends, since the constant lockdowns here in the UK made it impossible to see people.

I created a dog-walking business, aptly named the Barking Brigade, which Jonny designed some flyers and business cards for. The business went well, but it was for very little money.

Next, I jumped on the back of my friend Karl's venture, a sweets business called That Sweet Guy. I opened up a Newcastle branch as Karl was based in Leeds.

Selling pick-and-mix boxes delivered to people's houses in the local area was fun, but I was in no way passionate about it. In fact, I think it ended up contributing massively to my weight gain, having over 200 kilograms of sweets in the house constantly!

I knew that running a business was on the cards for me because I enjoyed it so much, but I just felt clueless as to what I would sell and what my niche would be. I had no real business experience, and I had no idea of where to even begin. As much as I wanted to run a business, I also felt quite scared as I'd heard so many horror stories about "the tax man" and all the potential fines you can get from HMRC for not filing things properly. To be honest, the whole thing petrified me!

One night, the thought crossed my mind that, being so passionate about crystal healing, I could start my own business by pairing candles with crystals and selling them online. It would also give me something to do in my spare time to ensure that my mind was occupied.

I was thinking small at the time, but the big dream was to have a platform to share my knowledge of crystal fundamentals, find a community of like-minded people who would enjoy meditating together, and, in that circle, finally be accepted for who I truly was.

So, with my last £250 in the bank earmarked for bills, I took a chance and bought a handful of candles from a friend, as well as a few rough crystals from a local shop. I remember when I was trying to think of a name for the business, my mind was blank as I sat in silence with my thoughts. I'm not a very creative person, so I really struggled.

Suddenly, I remembered my granda always used to say "gan canny" just before I left his house. It's a Geordie way of saying "Take it easy." I remember hearing his voice crystal-clear in my head as I was trying to think of a business name.

"Just gan canny!", the voice said.

And just like that, I launched my website cannycrystals.co.uk on my 34th birthday, 30th March 2021. I had absolutely no idea of the journey I was about to embark on and what would soon be possible for me in life.

To put all of that into perspective, at the time of writing this book, it's now 2024 and I have just over 100,000 combined social media followers. My podcast is constantly at the #1 spot in the UK for Spirituality and is listened to by 26,000 people weekly. I've just recently completed my 50,000th customer order, and I also launched the Canny Crystals Academy to help others come into their own power on their spiritual journey.

More recently, I've created a side business called Mani-Fest, where I can bring like-minded people together under one roof for a day of self-development seminars and workshops, with the first event planned for June 2025.

I've also worked with huge brands such as Chanel, Stella McCartney and British Vogue, and created a sold-out, one-night event at the Barbican in London with my business bestie and now friend, Francesca. We even went on to speak at Fearne Cotton's Happy Place Festival, not once, but twice this year. I've retired my mam so that she doesn't have to work and can help me out when busy. I manifested the car of my dreams, which is now sat on my drive, and I've had lots of other amazing opportunities come my way.

What could *your* life look like if you decided to harness the transformative power of spirituality, and navigate through its complexities?

Having reflected on this whirlwind journey, I've since come to understand that this was all my granda's parting gift to me, which sounds quite morbid but is true nevertheless.

None of this would have happened had he still been here with us.

His death led me down the path that I'm on today.

It was his absence that created a void, a silence, that forced me to listen closely to what was within me. I began to uncover pieces of myself that had been buried under the noise of everyday life. His passing became a catalyst that pushed me to explore passions I never knew I had, and to seek out experiences that I might have otherwise overlooked.

In a strange way, it's as if he's still guiding me, just from a different place. His influence, his lessons and even his stubbornness seem to echo in my choices and actions. It's almost like he knew that in his leaving, he'd leave behind a nudge, a gentle push to live a life fuller, richer and more in tune with what truly matters. And so, while losing him was a huge loss, it was also the beginning of finding myself.

I miss him every day, but I also thank him. For in his leaving, he left me a gift – the gift of becoming.

And for that, I am eternally grateful.

Chapter 2
Elevating Your Vibration

S ome of you may have read the last chapter and now have a few questions.

What is manifestation?

How do I get started with manifesting what I want?

What can I do to get out of the depths of despair, too?

Picture this: It's 8am, your alarm went off over an hour ago and you've just woken up for work, now an hour late. You jump out of bed, twist your ankle and then limp around your bedroom. You rush around your house getting ready, flinging clothes all over the floor in a desperate attempt to find something clean and ironed to wear. You rush your makeup but aren't happy with the way it looks. You burn your hair on your hair straightener and now you have a red mark on your forehead. You don't have time for breakfast and so you speed out of the house and run to your car with a grumbling tummy.

You jump in your car, start up the engine and hit the road. You've been driving for less than five minutes when you hit a traffic jam. You start cursing people, maybe even toot your horn a couple of times, and, just like that, someone pulls out in front of you at a junction and you smash your car into the side of theirs. Ouch!

What's happened here?

Have you just had an extremely unlucky morning?

Has someone hexed you?

Is your ex sat at home with your voodoo doll?!

No, what's happened is that you've fallen into a downward spiral of negativity and your vibration has lowered. That's all it comes down to.

I'm sure you've had a morning similar to that above – I know I have. Back in 2021, I bought tickets to the October Scarefest at Alton Towers from someone on a Facebook group, and off me and my friends went for the weekend. From the car park to the entrance gates, the heavens opened, and we all got drenched. It was torrential! One of the park staff scanned our tickets and a great red X came up on his machine screen – the tickets had already been scanned! Luckily, he still let us in, but over the course of the day, in the nine hours we were there, we managed to get on just four rides.

Soaking wet, we got back to the car park at around 6pm, absolutely starving for having not eaten, only to realise that my car was no longer in the space that I'd parked in. Panicking, I started to press my car key, hoping that my car lights would flash and illuminate where it was. And just like that, I looked down to the bottom of a nearby bank, and there was my car, crumpled against a pile of gigantic rocks. I'd mistakenly left my handbrake off and my car had rolled down the hill, slashing my front two tyres in the process.

After ringing for a recovery truck, the five of us had now been sitting in my car soaking wet and freezing cold for around seven hours. It was now 1am and there was a distinct wet-dog smell in the air. Other than my car, the car park was empty, and as the lights of the recovery truck came around the corner, we all breathed a huge sigh of relief. Apart from that, the fun wasn't over yet...

As we were dropped back at our accommodation, Jonny went to open the door and go inside whilst the recovery company unloaded my car onto the drive. I looked away for a split second before seeing my car come speeding off the ramp of the truck as the guy reversed it, crashing into a brick wall behind us.

As I stood there in horror, I could hear an alarm in the distance, and Jonny shouted over to us, "The security alarm is going off, and we don't have a code!"

You know those times in life when you feel like you're on a hidden camera TV show? This was one of those!

The next day, I rang for an emergency tyre fitter to come and change my wheels. As he started up his engine, his van battery died, and I had to bump him from my car. I felt cursed! I just wanted to get home. I didn't care how much it cost me, all I wanted to do was hit the road.

Unpacking my suitcase later that afternoon, I could smell a really familiar, yet pungent scent. As I started loading the washing machine, my fingers gradually started turning purple with each garment I popped inside. I then realised that my purple shampoo had exploded in my case and was now covering most of my clothing.

I wanted to go to bed and sleep for a week! I vaguely remember crying myself to sleep that night thinking, "How shit is my life? I'm so stressed and can't cope with all of this on top of everything else!"

Looking back at my mindset from the time this happened, I was still quite unhappy in life. I was trying to run my own business, Canny Crystals, while working full-time in the NHS. I had finally reached the point of burnout. I vowed to myself there and then that I would never allow myself to reach this low point again.

There's an old saying that goes, "Life has a way of kicking you when you're down," and that's exactly what happens when we get stuck in a rut.

When you get onto such a negative frequency, you attract more things to be negative about.

The Law of Attraction

Let's start with the basics, using an explanation known to many as the "Law of Attraction." The Law of Attraction is a philosophical concept suggesting that positive or negative thoughts bring positive or negative experiences into our lives. The belief is based on the idea that people and their thoughts are made up of pure energy – just like everything else on this planet – and through the process of like-energy attracting like-energy, we can improve our health, wealth, personal relationships and potentially every other aspect of our being. Essentially, it suggests that, by focusing on positive thoughts, we can bring about positive results.

Understanding and leveraging this powerful law can empower us to manifest our desires. By envisioning our goals as already achieved, we can attract the necessary circumstances and opportunities to make them a reality.

What happens if we turn our backs on this, choosing instead to navigate our days without that compass of our intentions?

Imagine standing at the crossroads of opportunity, but with our eyes closed to the paths unfolding before us. Without manifestation, we risk becoming drifters, carried by the currents of circumstance rather than steering our course through life's possibilities.

Failing to manifest our desires doesn't just mean missing out on achieving our goals. It leads to a deeper, more insidious stagnation. When we don't actively envision and attract our aspirations, we anchor ourselves to the status quo, and over time, this inaction breeds a sense of helplessness, a belief that our desires are out of reach and that the life we dream of is reserved for others, not for us.

Understanding and leveraging the Law of Attraction isn't just an option for those who wish to enhance their lives – it's a crucial strategy for anyone avoiding unfulfilled potential and unrealised dreams. By choosing to manifest, we choose to embrace the possibilities that life offers and step toward the future we desire rather than just watching from the sidelines.

Think of it as standing at a crossroads where each path represents a choice: One leads you to harness the power of your thoughts and the other to continue without change. Every day, we make these choices, often unconsciously. Consider the profound shifts that could unfold in your life if you chose to engage with the concepts of vibrational energy and manifestation.

What would your life look like if you decided to raise your vibration daily?

How would your relationships transform?

How would your health improve?

Would you find more joy in the mundane?

Now, picture the alternative: remaining on your current path without tapping into the immense potential of your own energy. Life might continue as it is, but what opportunities for happiness and fulfilment could you be missing out on?

Since reading *The Secret*, I've researched manifestation and our energetic vibration like you wouldn't believe, and trust me when I say this – it totally makes sense!

Everything Is Energy

Back in the olden days, way before many of us were even born, Einstein once famously said:

"Everything is energy, and that's all there is to it. Match the frequency of the reality you want, and you cannot help but get that reality. It can be no other way. This is not philosophy, this is physics!"

Einstein was clearly onto something back then – and he's one of the greatest physicists of all time! Who are we to argue with Albert Einstein?!

So, what exactly did he mean when he said "everything is energy"? Let's examine this in a bit more detail, starting with frequency. Our energetic frequency as human beings is naturally joyful and happy, but we rarely hook into that state because we let our habitual way of thinking about things drive our natural frequency down. We get stuck at lower levels of energy and just continue plodding along, as though this is what's meant to be and we have no say over it.

We need to start working on changing that. Smile more, be nicer, breathe and accept things, stop beating yourself up, relax, enjoy, laugh.

From time to time, we'll obsess for hours over something we did or didn't do – but what if you just chose to let it go instead? Acts like these immediately change our frequency. They move us from that energy of resistance, fear and worry to one of trust, acceptance and love.

When Einstein talks about matching the frequency, he means that everything we desire has a frequency set point. All beings, all things in the Universe, vibrate at a certain level.

Occasionally, you may experience anger or find yourself feeling a little flat. These emotional states vastly differ from the feelings of pure ecstasy or the serenity of joy. Scientific research has revealed that emotions ebb and flow within our bodies and dissipate after about 90 seconds[1]. This is why, when an event triggers an emotional response, that initial surge of feelings typically subsides in just a minute or two. This allows us to fully experience the emotion, but then also to promptly let it go.

But do we always let it go? Absolutely not!

Instead, we can hold onto it for days in our heads. We'll call up our parents and complain. We bitch to our friends. We get upset about something, and that sets us off about something that happened a week or a month or a year ago. We get stuck in patterns of thought and then regenerate all of the negative feelings associated with it.

Creating Your Own Happiness

In one of my last jobs working in the NHS, there was a colleague who didn't pull his weight in terms of the workload. This had a knock-on effect on the rest of the team. Before we knew it, everyone was slagging him off on a daily basis! I would often find myself in the thick of these discussions, and the more I got involved, the more irate I became over the whole situation.

Over time, I started to realise that work was dragging me down with negativity. I would resent getting out of bed in the morning knowing that I would face another day of doom and gloom. I wasn't self-aware enough at the time to acknowledge that I was adding to this feeling of despair by joining in with the discussions about workload and my colleague's lack of input.

This went on for weeks, probably even months, and eventually led to me applying for other roles. I felt defeated, overcome with a sense of anger, irritation and bitterness towards him. My vibration was so low, it may as well have been in the depths of the sea! Deep down inside, I knew that I wasn't that person. I knew I had to break free from the other colleagues around me to escape the endless cycle.

This is the kind of frequency we want to work on changing. It does require some self-awareness and a bit of work so that you don't get swallowed down the rabbit hole, but with patience and persistence, you will get better at it.

When we work on the frequency of our vibration, things slowly start to shift in relation to our relationships, opportunities, conversations, possibilities and our actual lives. You'll sharply start to realise that you *do* have a say in your own life, and not everything has to be dictated by other people.

When you start to manage your own frequency, you'll stop expecting it to be fulfilled by others and learn that *you* create your own happiness. As another example, I went years thinking that I could seek validation from friends and family by owning a Range Rover. Writing this down now, I realise how stupid this sounds! I guess I wanted to show off, and, to me, owning this car meant "success."

It'll be no surprise to you, however, that when I was finally able to purchase one for myself in 2023, I felt no different inside. Sure, there was a little buzz when I collected it from the showroom, and the first few times I drove it to my mam's house or took my friends for a spin in it. I'd worked super hard to allow myself to pay for it – but it made me no happier.

I wasn't in a state of pure ecstasy as I assumed I would be. Why? Because I was constantly seeking validation, expecting my frequency to rise because of other people.

Let me set the record straight here: We create our own happiness. Embracing this vibration allows you to release all expectations and demands. Your own thoughts are the sole architects of your life. Mastering the art of thought transformation is key, and once you do this, you'll find that not only does your vibration shift, but your entire world follows suit, too.

Energy is made up of vibrating atoms and molecules. You yourself are a living energy field! Your body is composed of energy-producing particles, and they're all moving in constant motion. So, like everything and everyone else in the Universe, you are vibrating and continuously creating energy.

Research has shown for a long time that our thoughts and behaviour affect the rhythm of our bodies[2]. For example, anxious thoughts trigger the release of stress hormones that stimulate your heart rate to speed up or slow down. The sound vibrations of music, for example, affect your thoughts and emotions, and so on. Vibrational energy experts have found that our behaviour and thoughts can also alter many smaller rhythms within us, and over the years, have suggested many ways to elevate the vibrations in your body and your life. There are so many ways to raise your vibrations, and I'm hoping that the following chapters in this book will all culminate in actions to do so. It's all about raising your vibration and matching the higher frequencies of happiness and joy that lie all around us.

Frequencies

Let's think about some frequencies that we know exist but can't be seen with the naked eye, such as infrared.

When you point your remote at your TV and press a button, the infrared travels through the air at the speed of light and changes the channel like magic. You don't see it going through the air, but the molecules in the air move out of the way to allow the infrared beam to travel from the remote to the TV. You don't physically see any of that with your eyes, but you trust and know that it happens.

Take the Internet or your phone as another example. These used to be wired devices, so all information off the Internet would be sent to your device via a wire or cable, and your phone would work in the same way. Now, everything can be done wirelessly.

You can open up a website on your phone, get texts, take calls, send emails – the list is endless. All of this information travels through the air without you seeing any of it with the naked eye.

If you can get into this mindset and know that these are things on a frequency that we can't detect, I'm hoping that you can understand that your thoughts are of a similar frequency.

You hear your thoughts in your head daily, but nobody else hears them. Does that mean they only exist inside of your head?

No, of course not.

Your thoughts are flying out into the universe constantly – you just can't see them.

Another thing is that frequencies are magnetic – whatever frequency those thoughts are that you're putting out, they're going to attract like-minded things to them. This is how we use the Law of Attraction to attract opportunities and possibilities to us in life.

There are thousands of videos on YouTube and playlists on streaming services like Spotify that feature different frequencies designed to align you with various frequency tones. For example, a sound played at 40 hertz has been used in Alzheimer's therapy studies to stimulate an increased neural response and fight symptoms of dementia. It's also been linked to gamma brain waves and the stimulation of memory[3].

Another example is that sound played at 285 hertz is considered instrumental in the healing of cuts, burns and other wounds across the body[4]. The 285 hertz sound frequencies activate the body's cellular regeneration, encouraging it to heal itself in the event of an injury. Hospitals in the 1940's even played this frequency across their wards to help heal patients faster[5]. This isn't just me chatting shit. This is literal science!

Whether I'm sitting packing website orders in my office, out for a walk with my dog or even relaxing in the bath, I'll pop on a frequency that'll benefit me in some way. If a simple sound played at a simple frequency can have this effect on the human body and the brain, what else is possible? There are frequencies to help you in any situation. Frequencies exist to open your mind and body to happiness, love, abundance, luck, releasing fear and negativity...the potential is limitless!

Just like how a lie detector can detect frequencies in the body, your body produces certain frequencies when it feels different things. Positive feelings all give off a frequency of around 400 hertz, which tend to be things like gratitude or kindness, moving up to 500 hertz for emotions such as love, compassion and joy. 600 hertz would be akin to peace and contentment, and then 700 and above would be pure enlightenment.

When you compare this information to negative feelings, the frequencies are markedly different. Everything negative is under five hertz. Whether that be pain, fear, irritation, pride or jealousy. By feeling these feelings, you're emitting a low frequency.

I like to refer to others who emit these low frequencies as "mood hoovers" or "energy vampires," and that's exactly what they're doing to you by you being around them – just like my colleagues back in that role in the NHS. They're lowering your frequency and draining you of all positivity. We're said to be the product or accumulation of the five people we spend most of our time around. Give this some thought right now. Are the five people you give the most of your energy to high vibing? Or are they sucking the life out of you, quite literally?

My principle for raising your vibration is quite simple: Surround yourself with high-frequency feelings as well as people who emit those high-frequency thoughts, and you'll attract better things in your life.

The Manifestation Mindset

Once we get onto this higher vibration, we achieve what I call a "manifestation mindset," whereby situations, experiences and opportunities will be magnetised to us and we can receive them effortlessly.

It involves adopting a specific mindset that focuses on consciously creating and attracting what we desire rather than passively accepting or reacting to external circumstances.

There are seven key aspects or steps to a manifestation mindset.

Number one, and probably the foundation of all of this work, is to have belief in the power of your thoughts. Simply recognise that your thoughts have the power to shape your reality, and that your predominant thoughts and beliefs influence the outcomes and experiences they attract.

Number two is to have clarity in our intentions and desires. This involves having a clear understanding of what you want to manifest in your life, setting specific and achievable goals to achieve that desire and being able to articulate your desires with clarity. What is it that you want? How do you plan to get there? Why do you want that goal? What would it mean to you? By being precise about what you want to manifest, you can focus your energy and intentions in the right places, attracting those specific outcomes into your life.

Number three is to keep a positive focus and practice gratitude. Cultivating a positive mindset by focusing on gratitude, appreciating what you already have and keeping optimistic even in the face of challenges is paramount. By adopting a positive outlook, you're able to raise your vibration and attract more positive experiences. Gratitude practices, such as keeping a gratitude journal or expressing daily appreciation, help us shift the focus towards abundance and create a positive energetic alignment with our desired manifestations.

Number four is to utilise visualisation and affirmations. One of the most powerful things you can do in life is engage in visualisation techniques to manifest desired outcomes. This involves creating vivid mental images of what you want in life, engaging the senses and feeling the emotions associated with achieving those goals. Affirmations complement visualisation, as positive and present-tense statements reinforce the belief that the desired outcomes are already present in your life. This combination helps program the subconscious mind and align it with the manifestation process.

Number five is to let go and have faith and trust in the Universe. Releasing attachment to the outcome and trusting that the Universe will align with our intentions is often referred to as "letting go and letting the Universe handle the details." While setting intentions and taking inspired action is important, a manifestation mindset also includes trusting that the Universe will deliver, often in unexpected and surprising ways. This mindset shift allows for greater flow and openness to receive our manifestations.

Number six is to meet the Universe halfway by taking inspired action. This is all about recognising that manifestation requires you to take action and actively take steps toward your goals and desires, following any intuitive guidance and opportunities that arise.

Many of us will put forth our intentions and wishes for the future, and then not act upon them. There's such a fine line between trust and letting go, and taking action towards our goals. Inspired action refers to taking steps that feel aligned and guided by intuition or inner wisdom. It involves being proactive, seizing opportunities and following through with actions that are in harmony with our desires.

Taking action not only demonstrates commitment, but also signals to the Universe that you're ready to receive your desired manifestations. Nobody wins the race sat at the start line, visualising – sooner or later, you're going to need to move your feet!

Last but not least, number seven is to engage in self-reflection and personal growth. Self-reflection plays a significant role in a manifestation mindset. It involves identifying and releasing resistance, limiting beliefs and negative thought patterns that hinder the manifestation process. Through self-reflection, we can become aware of any inner blocks or subconscious beliefs that are incongruent with our desires.

Personal growth practices, such as mindset work, meditation or journaling, help in ridding ourselves of these limiting beliefs and aligning ourselves with a higher vibrational state.

The Human Brain

Our brain is an amazing part of our body, but it tends to distort reality and has done so since you were a child. The brain receives over 400 billion bits of information every second. Take that in for a moment – 400 billion bits of information every second! To put that into context, it would take 600,000 average-sized books just to print 400 billion full stops!

So what does the brain do? It filters out all the crap.

"I'll take that bit of info from here, and this will fit nicely over here with my relationships, and I can use this info over here to make money..."

Once it's all filtered, the brain leaves us with around just 2,000 bits of information per second that we actually process through our senses. What we actually process and take in is just half of 0.0001% of all that our brain physically processes[6]. I find that fact actually fascinating!

Get a pen and some paper and make a dot with your pen point, I can do roughly five to six of these every second. Assuming each dot is a piece of information that my brain does process, then to make as many dots on this paper as your brain does in one second would take me just over seven minutes. If I was making a dot for every bit of those 400 billion bits of information, it would take me 821 years just to reproduce one second of what the brain receives!

Our brains contain a network of neurons that we call the Reticular Activating System (RAS), and this plays a pivotal role in this scenario due to its function as a filter for incoming data based on what you consciously or subconsciously decide to focus on. This directly influences the kind of experiences, people and opportunities you become more aware of and engage with in your daily life.

If your thoughts, focus, and attention lean towards negative outcomes, worries or fears, the RAS will filter information and highlight experiences that align with this negativity. This doesn't mean the RAS causes bad things to happen directly. Instead, it makes you more prone to notice, react to and remember those negative events. This can create a feedback loop where negative thinking will end up perpetuating itself, making it seem as though you're attracting more and more negativity into your life. You're more likely to notice what goes wrong, overlook positive opportunities and interpret situations negatively when you get stuck in this loop.

On the flip side, when you focus on positive outcomes, goals and the belief that you can achieve whatever you desire, the RAS helps you become more aware of opportunities, resources and information that support those positive beliefs and goals. This focus on positivity can make you more likely to recognise and seize opportunities that you might have otherwise ignored. It can also encourage a more positive interpretation of events and interactions, contributing to a virtuous cycle of positive experiences and outcomes.

By consciously directing your focus towards what you want to achieve or how you want to feel, you can effectively train your RAS to highlight information and opportunities that resonate with those goals and desires. This is why we should always try to make a conscious effort to focus on the positives in our lives.

I'll use an example which I use with my Academy members, whereby I ask them to carry out a little experiment from the book *E-Squared* by Pam Grout. For the next 48 hours, I'd like you to look for certain things – in this case, green cars. They're not very common, most cars here in the UK are white, black, silver, blue or red, but you barely see any green cars. I want you to make the following conscious intention: "I intend for the next two days of my life to actively look for green vehicles." Nothing special is required here, I just want you to use your eyes and look. Notice if your conscious intention has made a difference in the amount of green cars you see.

This is what I meant when I mentioned earlier about the 400 billion bits of information that your brain sees. You probably see green cars all the time, but your brain doesn't bother to process them because they're not relevant or play any part in your life. But once you start giving them attention, you will see them everywhere: in real life, on TV, in magazines, on Facebook or Instagram...

If you can start to see green vehicles in your life, just think of what you can do if you give your attention to what you actually want in life. If you give your attention to money, you'll see money-making opportunities that may have simply passed you by any other time. If you give your attention to love, you might catch the eye of your dream partner. If you give your attention to your career, you may just find the job opportunity that you've always dreamed of.

It's all possible, if you just give your thoughts to it.

What will you give your thoughts to?

Let's go back to the story I told you at the beginning of this chapter about waking up late for work. So now, with what we know, picture this: It's still 8am, you've already overslept again, but this time your phone is ringing. You answer your phone and are told that you've won £1,000,000 on the lottery overnight. You still jump out of bed and twist your ankle, but you don't care. You still rush around getting ready but aren't fussed about how you look; you're just too excited to go tell people about your lottery win. You skip breakfast but don't even notice your tummy rumbling as you jump into your car.

You still get stuck in traffic, and you still hit the car that pulls out in front of you.

But guess what? None of this has fazed you!

Why?

It's simple: You're on a higher vibrational frequency.

Being notified about your lottery win has enabled you to elevate yourself way above your normal frequency, and therefore nothing can bring you down.

That's a very extreme example, but you can understand where I'm coming from with this. You'll start to see all of the opportunities and adventures that life has to offer because you're more receptive to seeing them. They've always been there. You've just not been open to receiving.

When we feel really happy, positive and thankful, it's like we're on a high energy level. In this happy state, it's harder for bad vibes or negative things to bother us. It's not that bad things stop happening to us. It's how we see and handle them that changes.

We start to see problems as chances to learn and grow, not just as something bad. This way of thinking helps us stay calm and happy, no matter what's going on around us.

When we raise our vibration and keep our energy high and positive, we find it easier to get through tough times with a smile on our faces and joy in our hearts.

I challenge you, after reading this chapter, to think of all the different ways that you can elevate your existence by raising your vibrations, whether that be through the following:

Meditation. Meditating regularly helps clear the mind, reduce stress, and elevate your vibrational frequency.

Gratitude. Practising gratitude in your daily life for both big and small things.

Affirmations. Using positive affirmations to rewire your thoughts for positivity.

Nutrition. Consuming whole, vibrational foods like fruits, vegetables and grains to enhance your energy.

Sleep. Ensuring adequate and quality sleep to rejuvenate your body and spirit.

Time in nature. Naturally harmonising with nature to uplift your spirit.

Dance. Dancing and movement can help release pent-up energy and raise your vibration.

Positivity. Spending time with people who uplift you and share your aspirations.

Yoga. Combining physical movement, meditation and breathing exercises to enhance spiritual and physical well-being.

New experiences. Seeking new experiences and challenges to grow and expand your horizons.

Digital detox. Limiting exposure to negative news and social media.

Letting go. Releasing past hurts and grievances to move forward with lighter energy.

Although it's not a comprehensive list, these are just some of the things that helped drag me out of that spiral of depression and anxiety I was in.

Implementing these practices into your daily routine can help raise your vibration, making you more receptive to manifesting your desires. It's all about creating a lifestyle that works for you, and supporting your positivity, growth and well-being.

As you ponder the teachings of the Law of Attraction and the science of vibration, challenge yourself to imagine a life where every thought and action aligns with your highest aspirations.

What if, starting today, you chose to live intentionally, with every thought consciously aimed at manifesting your desires?

The question isn't whether the energy exists, it's whether you'll choose to direct it to create a life of abundance and fulfilment. The power to sculpt your reality lies dormant within you, buzzing at the edges of your thoughts, waiting to be directed with purpose and clarity.

Will you step into this boundless potential, or will you watch from the sidelines as life passes by?

Activity

What can you do today to raise your vibration?

Choose two items from the list I wrote on the previous page and commit to giving it a go over the course of the next week. It'll help you if you incorporate these activities by habit stacking, which is pairing your new habit with a current habit that you already do.

For example, you could spend time in nature whilst walking the dog, or you could express gratitude whilst in the shower or repeat affirmations on your drive to work. Doing this will improve your ability to carry out these new tasks without feeling overwhelmed.

When we take on more than two new habits at any one given time, we drastically decrease the likelihood of continuing with them, as our minds begin to feel overloaded. Have you ever said to yourself, "I'm going to start the gym on Monday, eat healthy, get 10,000 steps in and start meditating!", and then find yourself fallen off the bandwagon by Wednesday?

This is why!

Which two new habits will you integrate into your life for the next seven days to help raise your vibration?

Chapter 3

Identifying and Releasing Limiting Beliefs

I magine you're about to build your dream house, the one you've envisioned for years, complete with every detail that makes it uniquely yours. However, the plot of land where you plan to build is cluttered with scattered bricks, remnants of a structure that once stood there. These bricks vary in size, shape and condition, representing all the beliefs that you've accumulated over the years.

Building your dream house directly on top of these scattered bricks without clearing them away first is similar to trying to cultivate a new, positive mindset on the unstable foundation of existing limiting beliefs.

Just as constructing a house on uneven, cluttered ground would lead to structural issues, unstable floors and walls that might crumble, attempting to build a new belief system on top of limiting beliefs leads to a shaky foundation for personal growth. Your efforts to advance, no matter how sincere, are undermined by the unstable ground beneath.

Clearing away the bricks – your metaphorical limiting beliefs – is *essential* pre-work.

It involves examining each belief, understanding its origin and assessing whether it serves or hinders your growth. Some bricks might be whole and useful, symbolising beliefs that support your aspirations and can be integrated into the new foundation, whereas others are cracked or broken, representing detrimental beliefs that need to be discarded.

This clearing process ensures that, when you lay the foundation for your new belief system, it's on clean, stable ground. It allows you to construct a sturdy, resilient structure (your mindset) which will be better able to support the life you desire.

Just as a well-built house can withstand the elements and provide shelter and comfort, a well-founded belief system empowers you to face life's challenges with confidence and enables you to pursue your goals without the weight of all your limiting beliefs holding you back.

This foundational work is critical to building a life that truly reflects your aspirations and potential.

So what are your limiting beliefs?

If someone asked me a few years ago what mine were, to tell you the truth, I probably would have struggled. Now, I see a limiting belief as something that blocks or inhibits your ability to move on with your life in that particular area.

For example, back in 2020, my biggest limiting belief was that "I can't be successful." I used to reaffirm that to myself because I didn't go to university, nobody in my family had been "successful" as such and I was coming home with a standard salary each month. I didn't feel like I was amounting to much, and I was simply working to keep myself afloat.

From that limiting belief sprouted so many others, such as "I can't earn more than £2,000 per month," "I can't progress in my career," or "I can't treat my friends and family because I don't have the money to."

I realised pretty early on in my spiritual journey that if I wanted to achieve my bigger goals in life, I'd have to move from that place of fear to a place of courage, and that meant it was time to face and work on my deepest fears.

Beliefs are stories that we tell ourselves over and over again. They usually stem and come from stories we were told when we were younger, as well as things we've learned through personal experiences across our lives. Many of these thoughts and beliefs won't even be true anymore, but if you let them, they'll restrict your thinking and chain you to that unconscious image of what and who you think you are.

As adults, we repeat these stories to ourselves over and over again via negative self-talk, and then again out loud to family or friends or whoever will listen to us having a whinge. When you do this, your stories and your limiting beliefs become your reality.

Let that sink in. You are constantly re-affirming your limiting beliefs without even thinking about them, and on a daily basis.

There are two labels for beliefs: limiting, which holds you back from taking action; and empowering, which moves you further towards your goal.

We know from science that we as human beings have around 80,000 thoughts a day, and roughly 95% of those thoughts are negative, redundant or the same as yesterday's. So how do we recognise a fact that is known or proven to be true against a limiting belief that stems from an incorrect conclusion?

Let's break this down:

A fact would be something along the lines of, "I own cannycrystals.co.uk," or "I'm Mart, and I'm 37 years old."

A limiting belief is something that could be changed, but I don't believe inside that it can, and so it stops me from achieving my goals.

Some of the most common limiting beliefs that I see in my community are things such as, "I'm too old to do that," or "I can't be successful in business because I failed the last time," or "I just can't seem to lose weight and keep it off."

These are all limiting beliefs and are the things in our lives that will keep us trapped and stagnant in that cycle, going round and round, over and over again.

Take the Law of Attraction as an example. Everyone has their individual beliefs and opinions about manifestation. Some believe that if you dream about something often enough, it'll eventually appear in your life. Other people believe that if you write your goals down and journal them out, eventually they'll come to fruition. Some people just believe that you only get what you want in life through hard work, determination and perseverance, and that manifestation is a load of woo-woo nonsense.

After understanding what limiting beliefs are and identifying them in our lives, the next crucial step is to actively work to transcend these beliefs.

But why is this journey of transformation so vital?

By removing our limiting beliefs, we unlock a reservoir of untapped potential within ourselves. Imagine suddenly finding the courage to pursue a dream you thought was unreachable. This could mean starting a new business, embracing a healthier lifestyle or even exploring talents you never believed you had. The liberation from these mental constraints allows us the personal and professional growth that previously seemed impossible.

Overcoming limiting beliefs significantly enhances your quality of life, too. It's like lifting a weight off your shoulders. You start to see the world through a lens of possibilities rather than obstacles. This shift in perspective can lead to improved mental health, stronger relationships and a more fulfilling day-to-day experience. It changes the "what is" to "what could be."

The transformation from shedding limiting beliefs doesn't just stop with you either: It creates a ripple effect that impacts everyone around you. As you become more positive, empowered and engaged with life, you inspire those in your circle to reconsider their own limitations. This collective uplift can strengthen communities, foster more meaningful connections and even spark movements toward positive change.

But the most tangible outcome of discarding limiting beliefs is the achievement of goals that once seemed out of reach. Suddenly, success in areas where failure seemed inevitable becomes possible! Whether it's breaking through income ceilings, achieving long-held career aspirations or even conquering personal challenges like public speaking or travelling solo, the removal of these beliefs paves the way for achievements that enrich your life story.

Identifying Your Limiting Beliefs

I'd like you to think now about your own limiting beliefs. To do this, you're going to need to think of your number one goal.

You might wonder, why start here? The answer lies in the power of prioritisation and clarity that comes from focusing on what matters most to you! Your number one goal isn't just any target, it's the summit of your aspirations, the peak of your personal Everest. Concentrating on that number one goal allows you to identify the limiting beliefs that have the most significant impact on your life. These are the barriers that stand between you and your most cherished dreams, and by targeting these first, you can make meaningful progress.

Your number one goal also often harbours your deepest doubts and fears because it's where your desires and vulnerabilities intersect. When we explore the limiting beliefs in this context, it'll reveal not just superficial doubts, but the core fears that shape your perception of what you believe is possible for yourself.

Focusing on this goal naturally heightens your motivation and engagement with the process of overcoming limiting beliefs, too. It's easier to commit to the hard work of self-reflection and change when the stakes are high and the rewards are personally significant.

So, ask yourself, what is it that you want to achieve in the next year?

How does having that specific desire make you feel internally?

What would *really* set your soul on fire?

Give it some thought: What is your number one goal? If it helps you, write it down and verbalise it. Proclaim aloud, "By this time next year, I'm going to..."

I'd like you to notice and get clear about all the facts around that specific goal, as opposed to your own limiting beliefs. For example, if my biggest desire was to earn £1,000,000 (pretty wild, right?), my facts around that could include how much I'm currently making or the fact that I'm able to make money from various different sources and opportunities, whereas my limiting beliefs might be saying, "You're not at that level yet," or "Life is going to be harder to manage at a turnover of £1,000,000," or "You don't have the capacity or ability to keep up with that kind of demand."

Really dig deep on this one and give some thought as to what it is that's holding you back and limiting you – or more to the point, what you're *allowing* to limit you.

Start to notice how you think and what you say in relation to your goals. Are these thoughts and words in alignment, or do they contradict what you want to achieve?

Remember that whatever you think is what you affirm to yourself. So the more you think about your limiting beliefs and the more you don't debunk them, the more you're bringing that reality to fruition.

Changing Your Limiting Beliefs

Do you find that you tell yourself the same stories over and over again? If you do, just ask yourself, "Do I really want to keep this story with this narrative, or do I want to change it?"

Whenever I set myself a goal, I sit in contemplation and notice all of the feelings and thoughts that come up within me. How you feel inside is everything when it comes to manifesting what you truly want in life.

Do you feel good thinking about your goals, or do you feel negative about them? If you feel good, then the goal obviously resonates with you. But, if for any reason you do feel negative about your goals, this would be an area to look at and examine further.

You can turn your negative thought into a positive one by stopping it in its tracks and asking, "What is the first step I can take today to move towards feeling more positive about this situation?"

The sooner you get your head around this, the more personal power and awareness you'll have in life.

In the last chapter, I spoke about how, in order to change your vibration and manifest your goals, you need to pay attention to the present moment. This involves being aware of how you're feeling, what you're saying and what you're visualising. Now, it might seem unrealistic to be mindful and present every second of every day. Still, the benefits are astronomical if you pay even just some attention to the present moment, for this is where we sow the seeds for our future selves.

I grew up with my family using statements such as, "In one hand and out the other," when talking about money. My mam would make little impressions of other mothers at the school gates, saying, "Ooh, I love me, who do you love?" whenever someone appeared to be even the slightest bit dolled up and dressed nicely. My dad constantly told me, "Big boys don't cry," whenever I appeared upset.

From these three seemingly irrelevant memories, I developed three limiting beliefs. One, that whatever money I earned would be taken from me, with the inability to save any of it. Two, that I shouldn't take care of my appearance or aim higher for fear of being ridiculed. And three, that I should always bottle my emotions and feelings up, and never speak about them publicly. These were the three of the worst and hardest limiting beliefs that I've had to overcome in the last few years.

So how do we work on – and change – these limiting beliefs?

Now that you know how to identify them, I'd like you to grab a pen and paper and brain dump any negative beliefs that you have, verbalise them aloud, and accept that they're fears of yours. Just saying them out loud will help you realise what's holding you back.

Where do you feel the pain or the stagnancy within your body?

Anytime I feel stuck doing this little activity, I think to myself, "What's stopping me from moving on further with my life?" This simple question helps me to answer internally with clear conviction about all of the limiting beliefs holding me back.

The next step to get rid of your limiting beliefs is to delve into your mind to find the source of them. Where did they come from, and how did they become your reality?

You need to determine what instilled those beliefs within you. We're influenced by many things in life, but mainly people: the news, social media, friends, colleagues and family all heavily influence what we believe to be true. Sometimes, our deepest fears are from traumatic encounters, childhood memories and even other people's fears that are projected onto us. It's time you connected the dots.

For example, I have a big fear, like many of us do, about spiders. Yet, there's a photo that exists of me as a small child holding a tarantula! At some point in my life, that fear has been passed onto me as a learned reaction and has grown to the point of me being so terrified of them that I wake the entire house up screaming at 3am just from seeing one in the corner of the bedroom, much to Jonny's delight!

I've done a lot of work around limiting beliefs in the last few years, particularly around wealth, whilst creating content for my Manifesting Money Masterclass on my online academy. The first session of this course is coincidentally all about removing those limiting beliefs from our lives. I didn't realise when I started this work how emotional I would get in the first hour.

I ask my students to sit and journal for five minutes about what the role of money was in their childhoods, asking questions such as, "Did you have enough to get by?", "What did your parents always say about money?", "What was their attitude toward money?", and "What felt awkward and uncomfortable for you around money?"

By doing this internal work myself, memories started flooding back to me about money.

One of the very first money memories that came to mind, for example, was back in 1992 at primary school. In particular, it was the day we were going to have the annual year group photo. Every single person in that photo is in a burgundy sweatshirt. Me? I was in a burgundy bobble knit jumper that I'm pretty sure either my mam or nan had made herself. Thinking back to that day, I vividly remember our headteacher pulling me to one side and saying, "Can your mother not afford a school uniform?" before taking me from the centre of the middle row and placing me at the very end, next to the teacher, who did her very best to stand in front of me to hide the fact I wasn't in the correct attire.

Another memory that came up was the fact that I used to get free school dinners. Those meals were hard for me. If anyone at school saw you with your free school meal card, you would get names shouted at you, you'd be tormented, bullied...I went through that until I was around 16 years old.

In secondary school, my peers would all have fancy planners in class. They would be going out skating or bowling on weekends. They would be meeting to go out for food in the evenings. I couldn't, because my beliefs around my family not being well-off made me feel bad about asking my mam to keep paying for all these outings.

I remember in 1999, when we went to France on a school trip, my mam scraped money together over several months to ensure I could go. I remember her sitting and crying when I got home about a week after returning to the UK. She had paid for my disposable camera to be developed and was upset that there wasn't a single photo of me. Most of the photos were blurry and taken from the inside of our coach, and I was unable to tell what each photo was actually of. Reflecting on this situation, I surmise this made her think, "I'd spent all this money on him and have nothing to show for it."

My mam always quoted the standard, "Money doesn't grow on trees," or said, "We can't afford that," and "Stop wasting your money" while I was growing up. These are all negative connotations I associated with a severe lack of money in my life until recently.

Back in 2022, when I started to work through these limiting beliefs, I started questioning what evidence there was to support that these beliefs weren't real.

I spoke with my fiancé, Jonny, about it all one day, and he suggested that this may be why I'm obsessed with free things.

If someone has furniture or anything similar on Facebook Marketplace and they're giving it away for free, I feel like running around the house with a tape measure to see where it would fit, despite not actually needing it in my life. If I see something whilst out and about, insignificant, little things like tennis balls, keyrings, random crap that I find on my walks, I'll keep them at home until Jonny eventually bins it.

Doing this work has made me realise that I don't actually need to do any of this. I have everything I need in our beautiful home right now!

Both mine and my mam's lives are so different now, 30 years on, but I definitely think I've held onto some of the feelings I mentioned above. I felt like I needed to speak with her to release these limiting blocks and beliefs one day, and so I called her up for a chat.

Admittedly, it got her quite upset because she didn't realise how much of my childhood I had just kept locked in my head and not spoken to anyone about since it happened. But everything started to make sense the more we spoke. Both myself and my mam are terrible at buying things for people we barely know. Someone I'll have met once or twice at the gym or at work will say it's their birthday and I'll walk in with a cake, card and balloons – totally over the top!

I connected the dots and came to the conclusion that this is because we never had money before, and we know how isolated we were because of that. It's almost like we're attempting to buy friendship, which is really fucking sad, I know, but it's opened my eyes as to why we're the way we are.

I expressed my concern that the only way I felt that I could raise my income was by working myself into the ground, just as she and the rest of my family had done over the years.

I told her that it was safe for me to earn money online, and it was possible for me to earn it in different avenues than just my standard NHS job, where I was slogging myself 40 hours a week for terrible pay. Because of this, within one month of having this conversation, I launched Canny Crystals and more than doubled my income!

I think she initially found all of this information quite hard to take in, and the more I spoke about it, the more upset she got.

Another thing is that I sometimes buy things I don't need, just because I have the money sitting in my bank. I sometimes feel like I need to spend it quickly because otherwise, the money will disappear, which isn't the case at all. I looked back at some of my purchases in the year previous to this insight and realised I spent £200 on a Ninja Air Fryer! Don't get me wrong, I use it more than I use the oven itself now, but did I need it? No!

Did I really have the money to buy it? No!

Did I buy it out of boredom and just for the sake of a lavish purchase and because I could? Absolutely!

Myself and Jonny live in a three-storey townhouse, and I hate plugging the hoover in downstairs, cleaning the whole house, getting right to the top floor and finding that the cable won't reach into the last two bedrooms on the top floor. So, last year, I also bought a new Shark cordless hoover. Yes, it's easier than running around the house and finding a socket, but did I really need to spend that much on a new hoover? No.

Did I buy that out of boredom and all for the sake of a lavish purchase and because I could? Again, absolutely.

Can you see where this is going? I buy out of boredom. I buy because I'm scared that money is just going to grow legs and walk straight back out of my account.

And these are the limiting beliefs and blocks I have that I worked on dissolving and getting rid of.

I felt bad when I got off the phone with my mam, so much so that I rang a flower shop local to her and got a bouquet delivered to her house to apologise for getting her so upset. Even that in itself was, ironically, me buying for the sake of buying and attempting to buy friendship. Of course my mam loves me unconditionally. Of course she's always there as a friend as well as a mother, but I always feel like I need to send a token of my love, which is nice, in a way, but I've come to realise it's what's holding me back from having more money. My limiting beliefs were causing me to spend constantly.

I journaled daily on these thoughts, asking myself questions about my limiting beliefs, really searching my mind for memories of where these all stemmed from. I wrote down underneath each thought how I knew that this wasn't true in my life today. And then, once I was ready to, I let them go by having that conversation with my mam.

But our beliefs aren't always created from things our parents said or did.

Social media is another way that limiting beliefs can develop in our lives. Instagram for example, is one big highlight reel. Everyone posts their best moments and leaves out the reality that life isn't always perfect. No one would want to work with someone who didn't have their life together, right? During my school years, I felt that everyone was simply accustomed to projecting the image of having it all together. Having feelings, experiencing negative emotions or struggling mentally was a sign of weakness, and bullies would take advantage of you if you ever even dared to express those insecurities.

Those were some pretty heavy thoughts. While this is all new to you, it may seem a little crazy to analyse our thoughts and understand what exactly shapes these limiting beliefs – but this work is needed!

Choosing New and Empowering Beliefs

So how do we determine our new empowering beliefs? Thankfully, this is the happy part of the process!

What new belief do you want to believe?

Because, ultimately, *you* get to decide. I, for sure, don't want to be stuck with these negative thinking patterns, so instead, I'm changing my beliefs to be more positive and in alignment with what I want to achieve.

It may take time for these new beliefs to sink in, so don't lose faith instantly. One way to speed up the process is to look for evidence that your new beliefs are true.

What works best for me is finding role models who fit these new beliefs I want to adopt. I found and followed people on social media who managed to create savings and investment plans for themselves. I sought out people who took care of their appearance and worked with what they were given, even though they were far from walking a runway. I admired those who spoke up about their own mental health battles and the struggles they were facing.

Finding these people online and learning from them helped me dissolve my own limiting beliefs that were imposed upon me by my family. These people proved to me that my new empowering beliefs are indeed true – and if they can do it, so can I!

There was once a widely believed theory that it wasn't physically possible for a human to run a mile in less than four minutes. This barrier stood as a symbol of the limits of human physical achievement. For years, athletes tried and failed to break this barrier, leading many people to think it might actually be impossible.

The theory surrounding the four-minute mile wasn't a formal scientific hypothesis, but rather a combination of physiological, psychological and sociological observations about human performance limits. Experts believed that the human body simply wasn't capable of maintaining the speed necessary to complete running a mile in four minutes or less.

This belief was shattered on May 6th 1954, when Roger Bannister, a British athlete, ran a mile in 3 minutes and 59.4 seconds! Bannister's achievement had a profound effect on the world of athletics and beyond. It demonstrated the power of psychological barriers and how breaking them can lead to a floodgate of further achievements.

After Bannister broke the four-minute barrier, more runners used him as a role model to achieve the same feat in quick succession, proving that the barrier was as much mental as it was physical.

The four-minute mile theory therefore highlights the importance of mental beliefs and attitudes in overcoming the perceived limits we place upon ourselves. It's since become a metaphor in various fields for breaking through difficult barriers and achieving what was previously thought to be impossible.

Find people who have overcome your fears and limiting beliefs to look up to as role models. It's one of the best sources of inspiration you'll ever receive to quash those negative thoughts you have.

Something that I also find helps me personally is to think of the worst-case scenario and how I'm going to overcome it. This may sound counterproductive, but when I finally come to terms with what the absolute worst-case scenario is, I realise I'll be okay if that happens, and it's not actually as bad as it seems. This simple way of thinking helps me to dissolve the negative chatter in my head telling me that I can't do it.

Worst Case Scenario #1

I change directions in my business and completely fail.

What does "fail" even mean? I create a product or offer a new service that no one buys? OK, so the worst case is that I go in a completely new direction, my audience loses interest and shrinks, no one cares what I'm doing and I make zero money.

Thinking this through practically, I know I can always come up with another product or offer and make money. I know that I have useful skills and relevant experience to earn money with. I won't exactly be broke and living on the street. And if I change my business to be more in line with what I want and no one is interested...well, I decided to start a business that I was passionate about and would help people – I never did it to be everyone's answer to everything! So, I'll be okay, and I'll survive. If anything, I'll even learn from the experience.

Worst Case Scenario #2

I overshare personal information. People judge me and leave hurtful comments.

If I'm being authentically me with good intentions and not hurting anyone, I can't help how people interpret what I say and do. There will always be people judging me. If it's not online, it's in real life. Being true to myself encourages others to do the same! I know this because it was from watching other people be raw and real on social media that gave me the courage and strength to do the same. I'll keep doing my thing for the few who appreciate it and block the haters if I have to!

I think about worst-case scenarios to help me realise that "I'll be okay" even if it does happen. Most of the time, the worst possible outcome isn't actually that bad.

As the last bit of advice, re-affirm these empowering new beliefs to yourself. Some may see it as stating a lie, but I see it as stating that what you know deep down inside can actually be true.

When you repeat a statement over and over again, it sends a very clear signal to your RAS, and it'll let it know that this is important to you.

You could repeat statements along the lines of:

"Everything always works out for me."

"Happiness is my natural state of being."

"I am a creator of my own life."

"Money flows to me easily."

"I am surrounded by love."

I encourage you to write out your own affirmations, customised and contradictory to your own limiting beliefs.

Addressing limiting beliefs can also be quite tricky for people who have deeply ingrained beliefs, meaning that some of their thoughts may be so deeply rooted in their psyche that they feel like indisputable truths. They may be reinforced by years of habitual thinking and external validation.

Overcoming these often means stepping out of our comfort zone, which can be frightening. The uncertainty of change can sometimes be more intimidating than the familiarity of restrictions. Environmental resistance can often play a huge part in this, too. Family, friends and society can sometimes consciously or unconsciously reinforce our limiting beliefs, offering resistance to change.

We as human beings may even subconsciously sabotage our progress due to an internalised fear of success or a belief that we don't deserve better. We need to accept that changing limiting beliefs is going to be a gradual process. Practise patience and persistence while affirming to yourself that small, consistent steps will lead to progress. Focus on one belief at a time. Break down the process into small, manageable steps and celebrate small victories to maintain that momentum.

Don't hesitate to seek professional help if you feel stuck, too. Therapists, life coaches and counsellors can all provide expert guidance tailored to your specific challenges.

By anticipating these obstacles and having strategies in place to address them, we can navigate the complexities of changing our limiting beliefs more effectively. The key is to maintain a growth mindset, understanding that setbacks are not failures but rather opportunities to learn and strengthen ourselves.

Releasing your limiting beliefs takes time and don't for one second think it's something that you do once and it's all put to bed! Once you've identified and addressed all of your current limiting beliefs, you will have to revisit them every now and again. You may even return to negative thinking patterns, and that's okay – we all do from time to time. The more consistent you are with working through these beliefs, the easier it'll become for you to identify and release future ones that come up, too.

Eventually, these new ways of thinking will become habitual, and before you know it, your limiting beliefs will have been smashed.

I worked through a lot of my limiting beliefs back in 2022 with Jude Daunt, my life coach, and I remember her telling me, "You'll always have limiting beliefs." I remember thinking, but I'm going to get rid of these, so how will I still have them?

But it's true, because once you crack limiting beliefs, you level up to the next part of your life, and new limiting beliefs are triggered and come into play. *Hay House* author Denise Duffield-Thomas always says, "New level, old devil," and that's definitely true in this case.

We might eventually break that barrier of earning £2,000 per month, but then our negative thought pattern shifts to, "I'm going to have to pay more tax," "More money means more responsibility," or "More money will change who I am."

For me, overcoming my limiting beliefs set the foundation for the beginning of my success. I was able to use my new empowering beliefs to practise and manifest the life of my dreams with a successful business, a bank account with savings that I never could have dreamt about, and the self-esteem and confidence to show up daily for the community I've built.

Have a play around after reading this chapter. Ask yourself, "What's stopping me from moving forwards?" Instigate that shadow work and look internally at what your blocks and limiting beliefs are, and then complete whatever's necessary to thrash them. It's the only way you can clear the rubble and build those new foundations for something bigger and better to enter into your life.

Let's face it – negativity will always overrule positivity. That's just the way it works in our brain. We latch onto negative thoughts more than positive ones because our brains are wired to focus on threats and potential dangers. This evolutionary trait, designed to keep us safe, can lead to a cycle of limiting beliefs. But by recognising and challenging these limiting beliefs, we can begin to reframe our thinking, foster resilience and open ourselves up to new possibilities and growth.

Imagine for a moment that you've discovered an old, dusty map in your attic, leading to a buried treasure you've always dreamed about. But here's the catch: Your path is blocked by numerous boulders, each representing a limiting belief that you've carried, perhaps unknowingly, for years. Every step towards your treasure demands confronting and moving these heavy stones out of the way.

How long will you let them obstruct your path?

What could your life look like if you started removing them, one by one, today?

The journey isn't merely about reaching the treasure; it's about the freedom and growth you experience with each step forward. The decision to engage with your limiting beliefs isn't just a choice. It's a commitment to unlocking your fullest potential.

As you reflect on the limiting beliefs you've uncovered, ask yourself: What if these beliefs are the only barriers between you and your deepest desires?

Each belief holds power, but only if you allow it to.

Imagine the liberating, exhilarating freedom that awaits when you choose to dismantle these barriers. Think about the joy, the peace and the fulfilment that comes from knowing you are no longer held captive by your own subconscious constraints.

Visualise yourself a year from now, having cast these shackles aside.

Who are you in this new chapter, and how has your life transformed?

This moment of introspection is your call to action, your cue to rise, challenge the status quo of your inner narrative, and step boldly into the life you've always imagined.

Activity

Releasing limiting beliefs doesn't need to be time-consuming. One short, effective activity you can do involves writing and reframing. This activity helps you identify, confront and transform your limiting beliefs into empowering ones.

Step 1: Identify your limiting beliefs.

- Take a few deep, cleansing breaths to centre yourself.

- Reflect on areas of your life where you feel stuck or frustrated.

- Write down the beliefs that come to mind. Be honest with yourself. These could be beliefs like "I'm not good enough to succeed," or "I can't make money doing what I love."

Step 2: Challenge these beliefs.

- Look at each belief and ask yourself, "Is this absolutely true?", "Can I think of any instances where this belief was proven wrong?", "How does this belief limit me?"

- Write down your responses. This process helps to weaken the hold of these beliefs by introducing doubt and highlighting their subjective nature.

Step 3: Reframe each belief.

- For each limiting belief, write down a positive, empowering belief that contradicts or transforms the negative one.

- Instead of "I'm not good enough to succeed," you might write, "I have unique talents and abilities that lead to my success."

- Focus on beliefs that promote growth, possibility and self-compassion.

Step 4: Create affirmations.

- Turn your reframed beliefs into personal affirmations.

- Start each affirmation with "I am" or "I can." For example, "I am capable of achieving my goals through hard work and dedication."

- Keep your affirmations in the present tense.

Step 5: Visualise and commit.

- Close your eyes and visualise yourself living according to your new beliefs. Imagine feeling empowered, successful and free from old constraints.

- Commit to repeating these affirmations daily, ideally in the morning and before bed, to reinforce these new beliefs in your subconscious.

This activity not only helps in releasing limiting beliefs, but also plants the seeds for new, empowering beliefs to take root. Consistency is key. Revisit and repeat this exercise regularly to deepen the impact of positive beliefs on your mindset and life.

Chapter 4

Easing the Resistance to Manifestation

Picture this: There's a beautiful plant that flowers each and every year in your garden, but this year it hasn't yet started to bloom. When you look down at your plant, you see dead leaves and crispy, brown buds at the end of each stem. So what do you do to ensure the plant survives and grows?

You cut the dead ends off, carefully trimming away the old, withered parts. You do this not to harm the plant, but to encourage the growth of fresh, vibrant blooms.

This process, though it might seem harsh at first, is essential for the plant to thrive, allowing it to direct its energy towards producing new flowers. Similarly, letting go of what no longer serves us in our lives makes room for new opportunities, growth and adventures.

One way to attract more into your life and manifest your desires is to avoid getting stuck on the outcomes. Letting go of the end result will really ease your resistance to manifesting your dream life.

Have you ever noticed how sometimes, the more you want something, the harder it seems to get it? It's like the Universe is playing a trick on you. But here's a secret: The Universe isn't being mean! It's just that sometimes, we care so much that we get in our own way.

Think about needing something. It feels tight and stressful, right? Now think about *welcoming* something. That feels more relaxed and open. When we need, we hold on so tight that there's no space for what we want to come in. Letting go a little can actually help us get it faster. It's like making room in your wardrobe for new clothes by giving away the ones you don't wear anymore – more on this later!

Letting go doesn't mean not wanting, it means not *worrying*! Imagine you order a pizza. You don't keep calling the pizza shop every five minutes to see if it's on its way. You trust that it'll arrive, and you go about your other business until it does. The same goes for the Universe. Place your order, then trust it to come to you.

Need is rooted in lack, a belief that something is missing. This mindset actually pushes away the very things we desire because it focuses on the absence rather than the presence of what we want. There's a curious law of life that says the less we grip onto our desires, the more likely they are to materialise. It's a paradox, but it's one that's played out time and time again.

When we shift our focus from scarcity to abundance, we acknowledge that there's enough for everyone, including us. This shift is crucial in releasing the need and easing resistance.

The Mechanics of Resistance

Resistance is an inner force that often manifests itself when we're about to step out of our comfort zone. It's a natural reaction to change or challenge. However, when it comes to manifesting our desires, resistance acts as a barrier. Imagine you're pushing a boulder up a hill – that's what resistance feels like when you're trying to manifest something!

Resistance can be thought of as the voice of our limiting beliefs. It whispers in our ears, telling us about our inadequacies, reminding us of past failures, and convincing us that our dreams are impractical or unreachable. The first step in overcoming resistance is to recognise that it is not an external obstacle, but an internal one instead.

Abraham-Hicks, a well-known name in the field of manifestation, introduced the concept of an emotional guidance scale. This scale is a tool to help you understand where you are emotionally and how close or far you are from the state of "allowing," which is the opposite of resistance.

At the lower end of the scale, you'll find emotions such as fear, guilt and despair. These are heavy, dense emotional states where resistance thrives. As you move up the scale, you encounter frustration, doubt and disappointment, which are lighter but still resistant states. At the top of the scale are love, joy and appreciation, emotions that resonate with allowing and manifesting.

Climbing this emotional scale doesn't happen overnight, but awareness of your emotional state is the first step. By consciously choosing thoughts that feel better, you can move up the scale, reducing this resistance.

Recognising the symptoms of resistance is important because you can't change what you don't acknowledge! Some of the most common signs that you're resisting would be:

Procrastination, which is putting off tasks that could bring you closer to your goal.

Overwhelm, which is feeling swamped and unsure where to start.

Self-sabotage, which is engaging in behaviours that move you away from your goals.

Rationalisation, which is making excuses for not pursuing what you truly want.

And lastly, physical symptoms such as stress, tension and fatigue can all be bodily manifestations of resistance.

Once you identify these signs in yourself, you can begin the work of addressing them through techniques such as meditation or journaling.

Understanding resistance is the first step towards disarming it. By recognising what it is, where it lives within us, and how it shows up in our lives, we can start to dismantle the walls we've built against our own success.

This resistance may be caused by emotional attachments, past experiences or even limiting beliefs. The process of easing these can be really transformative and quite liberating because letting go of resistance and negative beliefs is vital in your manifestation journey.

If we don't let go, these emotional attachments or past experiences act as barriers. If you're holding onto any doubts, fears or limiting beliefs, they can then counteract the positive intentions that you're trying to manifest. So by releasing those negative energies, you create a clearer and more receptive space for your desires to come to fruition.

Essentially, it's all about surrendering control. We know that manifestation requires a delicate balance between setting intentions, hoping that they one day materialise, but also surrendering and letting go of the outcome, leaving it open for all the different ways that it could show up in our lives.

When you hold on too tightly to specific outcomes, or if you're fixated on how things should happen, it can block the natural flow of the manifestation process. Ultimately, you're not letting the Universe decide how it comes to you.

Manifestation in Action

Back in May 2023, my local radio station was holding a competition to win Beyoncé tickets and an all-expenses-paid trip to Los Angeles, as well as a cruise. I already had tickets to the tour, but I thought, "I could really do with a holiday and some sunshine right about now," having not had one for the last three years. I also knew deep inside that if I was going to win anything, Queen Bey was going to help me!

Every day for two weeks, at any unannounced point between 6am and 10am, the radio station would play a sound clip of Beyoncé saying a random word which was extracted from an interview that she had done over the years. The winner of the competition would be the person who rang up the radio station on the day of the final clip and relayed the sentence back to them in the correct order.

You best believe my office was like Miss Marple's secret hideout!

Every day for that two week period, my alarm would go off at 5:30am, I'd have a shower, eat breakfast and head down to my office, where I'd turn on the radio and listen intently whilst working. Each day, when a word was spoken by Beyoncé, I'd write it down on a post-it note, and place it up on my office wall. I'm sure my admin assistant thought that I'd lost the plot at one point!

I knew from about day 10 which interview that these sound clips had been taken from. One of the words was "Glastonbury" and I distinctly remembered when she was talking about being the first black woman to ever headline Glastonbury. Just to confirm my thoughts, I went straight to YouTube and I found the interview. It was word for word the exact interview that my local radio station was playing daily!

I had it in my mind from that point on that I was the winner.

To solidify that I was going on this cruise, I remember going up to the top floor of my house one day and raising the blinds to let the sunlight in. I surrounded myself with a handful of crystals for luck and success, grabbed my sun cream, smeared it all up and down my arms, popped on ocean sounds with seagull noises on my smart speaker and lay on my bed, gently closing my eyes and imagining I was on the top deck of that cruise ship.

I could hear the chatter of people around me as the ocean waves crashed around the ship. I could feel the warmth of the sun on my skin as it tingled up both of my arms. I could smell the sweetness of the sun cream as it hit the back of my nostrils. In fact, I could almost taste the gin I would have been drinking had I been on the cruise itself!

In my mind's eye, I was there.

I held onto this vision for the next few days until the final day of the competition. I remember being sat in my car that morning for 2 hours and 45 minutes listening to the radio, adamant to win, before they played the final clip. When those phone lines opened up to allow people to call in, I had both my phone and my partner's, and was frantically dialling on both!

I got through, and they told me I was fourth in the queue to have a shot at winning the Beyoncé tickets, the trip to L.A. and the all-expenses-paid cruise.

I was on edge, sat in my car drinking copious amounts of coffee, surrounded by the crystals on my dashboard and with a flutter in my stomach.

The first caller introduced herself and when giving her answer, read the words back in the wrong order. My heart started skipping beats as I remember affirming to myself, "This is my time, I'm the winner!" The second caller pretty much read out word for word what the first had said, and so they moved onto the third caller. I was so close to winning that my head started pounding with over-excitement!

The third caller came on and relayed the interview quote perfectly, in the correct order, and subsequently won. As soon as they announced that she had won, they hung up on me.

I came back down to reality with a huge bump, to say the very least. I was gutted that I hadn't won, having put in so much time and effort every single day, having done the visualisation work and taking it to the extreme, and now I had to come to terms with the fact that this just wasn't meant to be.

To be honest with you, I felt a little deflated.

I could have sulked and moaned all day.

I could have eaten and drank my sorrows away.

I could have sat feeling sorry for myself and let it ruin the rest of the week.

But instead, for the rest of that day I did things to try and raise my vibration by listening to upbeat music, going out for a nice dog walk and seeing friends. Because I hadn't won the competition, I released that desperation I had of being on the cruise.

This completely changed my vibration. I picked myself up and got on with the rest of my week, putting the whole experience behind me, deciding to choose gratitude for what I already had in my life.

About a week after all this happened, I was sat in my office working away when my friend Francesca sent me a voice note on WhatsApp. At the time, myself and Fran were planning a big one-night event in London, but this was proving difficult to do as she had three small children under the age of six, and she also lives a good three-hour drive away from me.

So imagine the shock, delight and jaw-dropping moment I had when I listened to this voice note from Fran telling me that she had been invited on a Virgin Voyages cruise to sail around the Mediterranean, visiting places like Barcelona, Corsica, and Ibiza. She told me it was all-expenses-paid and she could take a plus one. She had initially asked her sister, but unfortunately she was unavailable, and so Fran had asked *me*!

Can you imagine how I felt in that moment, listening to that message?

I wanted to spend time with her arranging our one-night show. I wanted to go on holiday. I wanted to go on that cruise... and then to have that offered up to me on a plate was one of the wildest moments I've ever experienced in my entire life.

I couldn't believe it.

Was this because I had visualised and seen it all in my mind?

Or was this due to the fact that I had released the *need* for the cruise after I hadn't won?

I truly think that this amazing opportunity came my way because I had released all resistance to it actually showing up in my life. Instead of assuming it had to be delivered to me via a radio competition, I had opened up all the different avenues that this dream of mine could come to me!

Since this happened to me, I've now realised the importance of not being set on *how* something can show up for me and simply leaving those finer details up to the Universe to deliver.

What we tend to do as human beings is overdo the planning, and if it doesn't happen exactly as we decided that it should, or how we think it should be planned out, we either criticise ourselves or just believe that manifestation doesn't work. In some cases, we never come back to it ever again.

Manifesting our goals is a process that involves bringing our deepest desires to reality. It requires us to have a clear vision of what we want to achieve and a strong belief in our ability to make it happen. However, even with the best intentions and a solid plan in place, we can still encounter resistance along the way.

Resistance can come in many forms, and it can make us feel stuck, overwhelmed and unsure of our next steps. Fortunately, there are several ways to ease the resistance to manifesting our goals. Regardless of the source, it can be challenging to move past resistance and stay focused on achieving our goals.

Taking inspired action is one of the easiest ways to ease this resistance. Inspired action is action that comes from a place of alignment with our goals and values. It's an action that feels natural and easy, rather than forced or stressful.

Before taking action, we might take a few moments to connect with our inner guidance. This could involve meditation, journaling or simply taking a few deep breaths to centre ourselves. We can always ask for guidance on what steps to take next, and trust our intuition to guide us.

Big goals such as the cruise I spoke about can sometimes feel overwhelming, which can create resistance to taking action. To ease this resistance, we can always break our goals down into smaller, more manageable steps. This makes it easier for us to take action and stay motivated.

Being consistent is key. Set aside time each day or each week to take action toward your goals, even if it's just a small step. This helps to build momentum and creates a sense of progress that can motivate us to keep going.

Sometimes the path to our goals may take unexpected turns, but it's important to remain flexible and stay open to new opportunities and possibilities. Staying open may lead us to even greater success than we originally envisioned.

Letting go allows the Universe to work its magic, and that will bring you anything that's for your highest good, without you restricting yourself to how it's going to get there.

Cultivating a Receptive Mindset for Manifestation

When we focus on the *why* of what we want, we feel all the correct associated emotions.

If I ask you to close your eyes now and ask aloud that you want £1,000 in your bank account in the next hour, you'd get so fixated on *how* it's going to show up and might have thoughts such as, "I'm going to have to buy a lottery ticket!" Subconsciously, you're then affirming to yourself that if you don't buy that lottery ticket, there's no other possible way on earth that this £1,000 could show up for you.

Instead, we need to focus on the *why*. Rather than think about *how* it's going to get there, think about *why* you want that additional £1,000.

What would you do with this money in your bank?

Who would you tell when you received it?

How would it change your life to have that surprise income?

By thinking about why you want it, when you visualise and close your eyes, you're going to feel all the associated emotions, and your brain will start to think of different ways it can get that money to you.

It might be that a business idea pops into your head, seemingly out of nowhere, and you make £1,000 from that. It might be that something else happens that leads you down another route where you take that inspired action, and the money comes to you in that way. There are so many ways that the Universe can deliver this money to you.

I'm just using money as an example because that tends to be one of the most common things people want to manifest in life, but ultimately the practice of letting go just brings you into the present moment. When you release any attachments to the past or worries about the future, you become fully present and open to all the opportunities and synchronicities that arise in the here and now.

Manifestation happens in the present moment, not in dwelling on the past or the future. That's why I often preach about using mindfulness techniques. It's all about living in the present moment, in the here and now.

So often when we visualise, we try to picture ourselves in certain situations, and most of us visualise as if it's yet to come. We visualise ourselves in the future when, in actual fact, we should *be* in that visualisation. We should be feeling those emotions as though it was playing out in the present moment, in real-time!

You might have heard the saying, "Let go of what no longer serves you," thrown around quite a lot, but it can really help you with releasing and easing that resistance. Whether it's relationships, situations or beliefs that you want to let go of, it's going to create space for new and positive experiences to come into your life. When you release the old, you make room for the new to enter.

Releasing and Letting Go

One perfect way of doing this is by getting familiar with, and taking stock of, what you currently have in your life and then decluttering what you no longer need. When you release the old and give thanks to it, the Universe makes room for new things to enter it.

Every now and then, I like to work through my wardrobe, ridding it of any items of clothing that I either no longer like or no longer fit me. (Yes, my waistband is expanding daily!)

In doing so, I show gratitude and thanks to my clothes as I pull them out and bag them up for a local homeless charity. This seems like a peculiar thing to do, but I often lay them all out on my bed and say something along the lines of, "Thank you for all the times I've worn you – and thank you for keeping me clothed and warm, looking my best at all times." This is something that Marie Kondo does on the Netflix show, *Tidying Up*.

The first time I did this, I had an old coat that I'd simply outgrown. It was lovely, but I couldn't get it fastened any longer, so I made the decision to donate it. We were in the middle of winter when I did this decluttering exercise, and I knew that I needed a coat to keep me warm on my dog walks. Within minutes of me being grateful for all the usage I'd gotten from it, Jonny saw me cleaning my wardrobe and felt inspired to start to do the same to his.

He turned to me with a beautiful, padded jacket and said, "I'm going to get rid of this, I think I've only worn it once or twice, but I just don't like it on me anymore!"

I tried it on and the jacket fit me perfectly. It was so warm and comfy, too!

I made space in my wardrobe, showed gratitude and that space was filled with something new as though it was meant for me.

Decluttering your physical space can have a significant impact on your emotional well-being because letting go of possessions that you no longer need can symbolise the release of emotional attachments as well. This release can really help you to let go of the outcomes for your manifestation.

Manifestation involves trusting that the Universe knows the best time and place for the fulfilment of your desires, so you need to let go and allow yourself to trust that what you desire *will* come to you. Even if it doesn't happen immediately, it will happen when the time is right and when it's for your highest good.

Letting go of what you don't have or haven't manifested yet also allows you to shift your focus to what you're grateful for in the present moment. One affirmation that I use almost daily to help me release this resistance when manifesting is, "Universe, send me this, or something better!" By phrasing it like this, it's almost like having a "Plan B."

Being both aware and accepting of all outcomes is vitally important. Earlier, I spoke about attempting to manifest £1,000. What would happen if this didn't come to you? You'd just carry on with life exactly how you are right now, of course. Nobody died; nothing got worse than it already was. It just remains the same.

When you truly get to grips with releasing all attachments to the outcome, that detachment eases the pressure and anxiety around manifestation, which will allow you to approach the process with a sense of ease and flow. We get so stuck in that cycle of, "Oh my God, it's not going to happen to me," or "Why hasn't it come to me already? What am I doing wrong?"

When you come to terms with the "Plan B," you'll be able to truly detach yourself from the situation.

Rhonda Byrne, author of the book *The Secret*, constantly spoke about her three steps to manifestation: 1.) Ask, 2.) Believe, and 3.) Receive. This, right here, is the belief stage, because you're letting go and releasing to the Universe that you believe everything is going to come to you.

By incorporating these little practices into your manifestation journey, you're going to open yourself up to all the possibilities and allow the Universe to work in harmony with your intentions. By becoming aware of the thoughts and emotions behind the attachments that you want to release, you can acknowledge and accept them without judgement. You can understand that it's okay to have those feelings, and that it's natural to hold on to things from the past.

Journaling and writing down your thoughts and emotions can be a powerful tool for processing and gaining clarity on *why* you might be holding on to certain things. It can also help you identify any patterns or triggers so that you can see clearly what it is you truly need to let go of.

I'd advise you to consider forgiveness as part of the release process, too. When you forgive yourself and others for past mistakes or hurtful experiences, this helps to free yourself from the emotional burden associated with them. By forgiving, you're able to move on from the situation. And I don't mean just sweep it to one side. I mean *truly* move on. When we forgive something, we can let it go, and by releasing and letting go we're going to attract more into our lives. As part of forgiveness work, you can also talk to someone about your thoughts, because sharing these thoughts and emotions with friends or family can be really therapeutic. Other people can provide support, a fresh perspective or even guidance in the process of letting go.

As you release what no longer serves you, you're going to create space for new experiences, new growth and positive energy to enter your life. One way you might find easiest to do this is by writing yourself a letter of everything that you don't want to take with you into the month ahead, and by that I mean any feelings, emotions or anything that you've been trying to manifest that hasn't yet come to fruition. This could involve people or situations that you're no longer taking forward with you.

Writing a letter to release and let go can be such a powerful ritual for setting intentions for yourself, and it can also help to clear those negative energies and welcome positive change into your life.

Reflect and identify what you want to release – take some time on this. What is it that's holding you back?

Is it a person?

Is it a situation?

Is it something that you can easily put in the bin because it's a painful reminder?

It could be a photo of you and your ex-partner that's currently sat on your bedside table and you want to let go of it. It could be limiting beliefs or patterns, toxic relationships... anything that no longer serves you or your highest good. Be honest with yourself and identify the areas in your life that you wish to release, and then write your letter.

Use this journaling exercise to express gratitude for all the lessons that you've learned from the things that you'll be releasing. Be specific and heartfelt in your words and express your intentions for positive change. Focus on what you want to bring into your life and the qualities that you want to cultivate.

For example, if you're releasing fear, you might intend to welcome courage and confidence in your life instead. Consider including a section of your letter about forgiveness, too, either about forgiving yourself or others involved in the situation that you're releasing.

Once you've written your letter, read it aloud and allow yourself to feel the emotions connected to what it is that you've written about. When you're ready, you can choose to burn the letter as a symbolic and cathartic act of releasing these energies into the Universe. Or you can rip it up, flush it down the toilet, dispose of it, bury it – do whatever feels respectful to you.

Have trust and faith that the Universe is working with your intentions and everything will unfold in its own time. I often find that the ritual of writing a letter to release and let go can be quite an empowering practice for personal growth, as well as for positive change.

Letting go isn't about inaction. It's about taking mindful steps towards our goals while releasing attachment to the outcomes. It's about understanding that there's a flow to the Universe we can align with, and it requires a balance of effort and ease.

To let go effectively, we *must* cultivate trust: trust in ourselves, in the process and in the Universe. This trust is sometimes referred to as faith, which doesn't have to be religious. It can simply be a deep-seated belief that things will work out exactly as they're meant to in the end.

Reflect on past successes. Remembering times when things worked out unexpectedly will help you to realise the potential for positive outcomes. Use daily affirmations to reinforce your trust in the Universe. Phrases like "I trust the process of life" can be especially powerful.

Consciously decide to surrender your worries each day. This can be done through a mental note, a written statement or via spoken word.

It's important to balance action towards your goals with a state of being that's receptive and open, so set intentions – not expectations – when you begin a task. Do it with intention rather than a rigid expectation of the outcome. Try to enjoy the process, too. Engage in activities related to your goals because you enjoy them, not solely for the end result.

Understand what is within your control (your actions and efforts) and what isn't (the outcomes and timing). By practising these steps, you can align yourself with the rhythm of manifestation. Detachment isn't about giving up on your dreams; it's about living fully in the present while maintaining a hopeful vision for the future.

As you integrate these practices into your life, you might even find that what you desire comes to you with greater ease and often in greater forms than you had previously imagined.

The act of letting go isn't a one-time event but rather a continuous process. It's about gradually shifting our focus from a mindset of scarcity to one of abundance, from a heart clenched with need to one open and ready to receive. The stories shared, the strategies discussed and the exercises provided in this chapter are all designed to guide you into a state of allowing, where manifestation isn't forced, but welcomed with ease.

Manifestation is as much about the internal journey as it is about the external outcomes. The peace of mind that comes with letting go, the joy of living in the present, the serendipitous encounters that unfold when we trust – these are the *true* gifts of embracing this new paradigm.

As you read on, carry with you the wisdom of surrender, the courage to release control and the faith to trust in the unseen. Trust that the Universe is conspiring in your favour, that your desires are on their way to you and that each step you take is in alignment with your destiny. Invite more ease, more grace and more fulfilment into every area of your life.

Easing the resistance to manifesting our goals is a process that requires introspection, positivity and inspired action.

By identifying and releasing limiting beliefs, focusing on the positive and taking inspired action, we can overcome resistance and achieve our goals with greater ease. Remember to be patient and persistent, and trust in the process of manifestation.

As you contemplate easing your resistance to manifestation, consider this: Resistance isn't just an obstacle, but a guidepost pointing you towards deeper truths about yourself and your desires. Each moment of resistance offers a heartfelt opportunity to ask, "What is this teaching me?"

By embracing these lessons, you allow each experience to enrich and prepare you for the life you yearn to manifest. What if you viewed each setback not as a stop sign but as a detour sign, guiding you on a possibly longer, but ultimately more scenic route to your dreams?

Such a perspective could transform the way you navigate your journey, turning each moment of resistance into a stepping stone towards greater self-awareness and success.

Activity

Meditation can be a powerful tool for detachment because it teaches us to observe our thoughts and feelings without getting entangled in them.

Start with five minutes of deep breathing, focusing solely on the rise and fall of your breath. This calms the mind and eases tension.

Visualise your desire as an object floating down a river, moving gently away from you, signifying your release of attachment.

Practice mindfulness by fully engaging in the present moment, whether you're eating, walking or simply resting.

I've popped a Releasing and Letting Go meditation in the resources online section of this book, which you can download free at cannycrystalsacademy.co.uk/limitless

Chapter 5

Gratitude: The Power of Positive Thought

Imagine starting every day with the guarantee that it is full of gifts for you. The gifts aren't wrapped in shiny paper, however, nor handed to you by your friends or family. They're a smile from a stranger, a cup of coffee made just right or the comfort of your favourite chair. Every moment, life offers us an abundance. Recognising and appreciating those moments, big or small, is the true essence of gratitude. These moments hold the keys to true contentment.

As we search for happiness in big achievements and acquisitions, we can overlook the small wonders of our daily lives. Gratitude's power is in flipping the mental script from "not enough" to "more than enough." It transforms the way we see our half-empty glass into a glass that's overflowing, regardless of how much is actually in it, changing our perception from what's missing to what's present.

Gratitude is about embodying appreciation as a state of being, a way of seeing the world. It's like putting on a pair of glasses that suddenly brings everything into focus. Things you walk past every day suddenly pop with colour and meaning. It isn't just a word, nor is it about saying "thank you." Yet, the simple act of being thankful can lead us to a wealth of joy and optimism, which is what this chapter is about.

At its core, gratitude is an acknowledgement of value. It's recognising the good in our lives and understanding that this goodness is partially thanks to outside sources, from people to higher powers or even the Universe itself. It's about noticing the simple pleasures, acknowledging the gift of life and understanding that we're part of a larger interconnected web.

Consciously practising gratitude is like training a muscle. Our brains are hardwired to focus on the negative – it's a survival mechanism. However, research shows that gratitude can actually change the neural structures within our brains, making us feel happier and more content. Feeling grateful and expressing it releases dopamine and serotonin, the two crucial neurotransmitters responsible for our emotions, and they're what make us feel good. They enhance our mood immediately, making us feel happy from the inside.

Gratitude has been a central theme throughout history and across cultures, too. Ancient philosophies and religions from Greek to Native American traditions and from Buddhism to Christianity have long spoken about the importance of giving thanks. More than trained conduct, these practices are about sustaining a worldview that promotes well-being and harmony. By learning from these traditions, we can see that gratitude is a universal language that can bridge divides and enrich our modern lives.

I remember watching American sitcom TV shows, such as *Friends* or *Will and Grace*, whilst growing up, and in them, we often see the characters celebrating Thanksgiving or simply giving thanks for the food they're about to eat. This isn't widely practised here in the UK. Because of this, I always viewed gratitude as something that only religious people do, giving grace to God for the food on their plate like a prayer.

It's only since starting on my own spiritual journey that I've realised just how important gratitude is and how it can really change my perspective in my daily life.

Let's take this morning as an example. I woke up at 6am, had planned to get to the gym, do my food shopping, run a few errands, head down to my office and potentially do some housework once I returned home. As I write this, it's mid-afternoon, and other than having a shower, I haven't managed to do a great deal else!

I could beat myself up for not achieving anything from my to-do list.

I could feel anxious about time slipping through my fingers, having not done anything I said that I was going to.

I could find myself spiralling into a state of feeling overwhelmed.

Instead, I chose to write myself a gratitude list of five things to be grateful for, actually slow down and spend the morning writing this chapter instead.

"I am so happy and grateful that I didn't have to leave my house to start work and sit in that dreaded rush hour traffic," I wrote for my first sentence.

"I am eternally grateful that I can work remotely and have the pleasure of doing so in the comfort of my own home, with my family by my side," I continued.

Having this awareness of what I'm truly appreciative of made me realise just how lucky I am to be able to work for myself, which changed the focus from feeling like I was drowning in things to do to an attitude of gratitude for what this allows me to achieve.

Back in 2021, I found myself having such a down day. I was severely burnt out and lacking any form of energy. That day overlapped into the next day, and then again into the next day, and before I knew it, I could feel the pull of the downward spiral.

I knew it was time to practise what I was preaching, and after looking at my situation from an outsider's perspective, I sharply realised what had changed: I'd stopped writing down my morning gratitudes!

I'd become so busy in my full-time NHS job and in my attempts to run Canny Crystals in my spare time that I was jumping out of bed in the morning and starting work almost immediately. I would sometimes even respond to emails on my phone whilst in the shower getting myself ready.

I remember thinking to myself, "Surely my life wouldn't turn itself on its head just by me not remembering to practise gratitude on a daily basis, would it?" But this one simple practice was helping me start my day off right, by being grateful for every little thing in my life rather than starting it dismayed and becoming overwhelmed.

Once I had this realisation, not only did I start to write down my gratitude list in the morning, pre-empting the day ahead, but I would also put my journal on my bedside table so that, just before bed, I could give thanks to everything that actually happened throughout the day, no matter how big or small.

Daily Gratitude Reflection

To help cultivate this awareness, try this simple daily exercise:

Each evening, write down three things that happened during the day for which you're grateful.

Reflect on why these moments were significant to you.

Consider how your day might have felt different without noticing these moments.

This exercise trains the mind to spot and appreciate the good, transforming occasional gratitude into a habitual mindset.

Beyond dopamine and serotonin, practising gratitude can reduce stress hormones and even improve overall brain function by increasing neural modulation in the brain's prefrontal cortex. This area is responsible for managing negative emotions like fear and aggression. Therefore, gratitude not only makes us happier, but also less reactive to negative experiences.

In moments where you feel overwhelmed, you can try a little gratitude meditation. I start by finding a quiet place and closing my eyes. I take a few deep breaths to centre myself and then think of a person who has been kind to me.

I visualise their face and mentally say "thank you" to them, feeling a sense of warmth and appreciation. Next, I expand this gratitude outward to others in my life, to those who have supported me, and to those who challenge me.

I find that this short meditation, which only takes a couple of minutes per morning, helps not only in cultivating an emotional connection to gratitude, but also in reinforcing neural pathways associated with positive thinking and empathy.

Gratitude doesn't just make us feel better in the moment, it builds our resilience to stress and adversity, too. When we practise gratitude regularly, we develop a buffer against the negative effects of setbacks and disappointments. By focusing on what we have rather than what we lack, we're less susceptible to feelings of deprivation and are more equipped to handle life's inevitable challenges.

Developing a consistent gratitude practice is key to reaping its full benefits. This can be as simple as maintaining a gratitude journal, setting aside a few moments each day to reflect on what you're thankful for. Or, you can incorporate gratitude into your meditation or prayer routines.

Don't get me wrong. Some days I might not remember to fill in my journal or do my little gratitude meditation, but what I've got into the routine of is setting mental triggers and anchors that remind me to speak my gratitude aloud.

One of these triggers is when I get into my car. I use that action to anchor my thoughts back to my attitude of gratitude. As I turn the engine on and buckle up my seatbelt, I'm affirming things like, "I'm so thankful for my lovely car, and so grateful that I can afford diesel to be able to drive myself safely to wherever I need to go!" This helps me ground myself in the present moment and prompts me to think of all the positives in my life.

When we incorporate daily gratitude practices like these, we can transform our perception and enhance our overall life experience. Gratitude is deeply intertwined with the Law of Attraction, as it directs our focus toward life's positives, magnetising similar blessings to us. When we appreciate our current blessings, we emit positive frequencies that bring further abundance into our lives. This shift from scarcity to abundance invites even greater prosperity.

Manifesting often entails envisioning desired outcomes and emotionally connecting with them as if they were already achieved. Gratitude simply amplifies those positive feelings associated with our desires, smoothing the path for their materialisation into reality. Embracing gratitude as if the desired outcome is already ours elevates our vibrational energy, and that's going to attract corresponding experiences.

Practising gratitude extends beyond manifestation. It significantly bolsters our physical, emotional and mental health. I'm a big advocate for mental health having worked in that speciality for years in the NHS. Even just sitting with this present moment and thinking about one thing that we can be grateful for can seriously enhance our mental wellbeing.

Mentally, gratitude is linked to reduced depression and anxiety levels, fostering a heightened state of well-being.

Physically, it correlates with lower blood pressure, improved sleep and stronger immunity, which helps encourage healthy habits.

Socially, it strengthens connections, empathy and support in relationships, promoting forgiveness and reducing resentment.

Emotionally, it builds resilience, aiding us in finding meaning in challenging times.

Lastly, it enhances self-esteem, as focusing on our blessings rather than our lack cultivates a positive self-perception.

Having a strong gratitude practice is a transformative tool for a happier, healthier and more satisfying life. Below are six ways we can begin appreciating what we already have.

Maintain a Gratitude Journal

Daily, jot down three aspects of your life you're thankful for. These can be as basic as shelter, a nourishing meal or time with family. Recording them solidifies your focus on life's positives. This may seem like the simplest thing to do, and it only takes you five minutes per day, but truly connecting with that gratitude at such a cellular level will enhance everything you do for the remainder of the day. Just like anything with the Law of Attraction, consistency is key, so try and build this into your morning routine. If it means doing it whilst waiting for the kettle to boil, or whilst you're sat on the toilet or on your morning commute to work – wherever it suits you best, get it done, and I promise it'll set you up right for the day.

Show Appreciation

Expressing thanks to those who positively impact your life, perhaps through a message or thank-you note, can really elevate those feelings of thankfulness and gratitude that we have. Maybe someone moved over on the bus and made room for you to sit down, or someone told you that your hair looked nice today. Accept that and express thanks to them, because once we're in that high vibrational state, nothing can stop us. We start to attract all of these other scenarios and the Universe will start to deliver more circumstances similar to these.

Engage in Mindfulness

Try to dedicate moments in meditation or prayer to reflect on your life's blessings throughout the day. Sometimes we get so stuck on autopilot that we don't always see the blessings around us. For example, maybe someone makes you a coffee at work, maybe someone tells you that you've dropped something on the street, maybe someone sends you a text to see if you're OK… these might sound like little tiny things, but if we're not present, they could end up going unnoticed by us. By the time we get to the end of the day, we might think, "What a crappy day, what have I got to be thankful for?" when, in actual fact, we've just been gratitude-blind!

Affirm Positivity

Begin each day with affirmations of gratitude, such as "I cherish all the goodness in my life," or "I am thankful for my supportive circle." When we affirm such statements to ourselves, we change what's going on inside of our bodies. This takes no extra time because you can say these aloud whilst showering, whilst putting clothes on, whilst doing your makeup, etc. The best part is, you can make them up on the spot. So, right now, I'm going to affirm to myself that I'm super grateful for the opportunity to tell my story and share my knowledge with you all through this book, and that I'm so thankful for you all reading! Really connect with the energy of that affirmation.

Remind Yourself

Set reminders on your phone or computer throughout the day to pause and think of something you're grateful for. These small prompts can be a powerful tool to bring your focus back to gratitude throughout the day. There's an amazing free app that I use called Yapp! where you write down and create maybe 10 different daily reminders, like "I am so thankful for all the money that enters my life effortlessly," and at different points throughout the day, you'll get a reminder on your phone with one of those affirmations. It's a great way to anchor yourself back to gratitude.

Find Gratitude in Challenges

Try to find something to be grateful for even in difficult situations. This isn't about ignoring the negative, but recognising that challenges can also bring lessons and new opportunities. You'll have heard the phrase, "Every cloud has a silver lining." Take my story in Chapter 1 about my granda dying, for example. I was in the depths of despair when that happened. But now, five years later, I can sit here, talking about his life and showing true appreciation for the gift he gave me by dying. None of this would have happened had he not passed. Obviously, I would love nothing more than for him to be here right now, because I miss him dearly, but had he not passed, I would probably still be working in the NHS struggling to make ends meet, and I certainly wouldn't be sat here right now writing this book for you. Every cloud has a silver lining – trust me on that one – and you can find simple gratitudes in even the darkest of moments.

By embedding these practices into your daily life, you cultivate gratitude, fostering positivity and contentment even through tough times. These methods are just some of what we'll delve into further throughout this chapter.

31 Days of Gratitude

Embarking on a journey of change can often seem intimidating, which is why I often prefer to break all of this down into 31 manageable pieces that can make a world of difference, allowing you to maintain and even expand upon your gratitude practice well past the initial 31 days.

Consider the book *The Magic* by Rhonda Byrne, which proposes the daily task of acknowledging 10 points of gratitude, totalling 280 across 28 days. This might seem overwhelming, but it is the challenge's goal to broaden your perspective on gratitude and its myriad possibilities in enriching your life.

Consistency turns action into habit, shaping who we become. By regularly engaging in gratitude, it becomes a fundamental part of our daily existence, harnessing the energy that gratitude infuses into our lives. So, by attempting to continue your practice over 31 days, what you're actually doing subconsciously is building it into your daily routine and having it turn into an effortless habit.

I challenge you to integrate gratitude into your daily activities, making it a fundamental part of your lives. It's about shifting from a scarcity mindset to one of abundance.

By normalising abundance and positivity, we open ourselves to transformative energies, enabling us to achieve our desires. Gratitude has the power to convert simple moments into pivotal experiences – it all depends on how we perceive them.

If you can, I want you to take a pen and either a journal or notepad right now, and I want you to simply write down these three journal prompts:

1. Reflect on what brought you joy yesterday.

2. Consider what self-loving action you can take today.

3. Acknowledge something you're thankful for today.

Once you've noted these questions in your journal, I want you to take a moment to settle into your surroundings, whether that's in bed, at a desk or elsewhere, and simply check in with yourself.

Breathe deeply and ponder these three statements. You might choose to write down your responses, note them electronically or even just contemplate them in your thoughts.

Writing down your reflections can be particularly comforting on days when you feel low, serving as a reminder of positive moments.

If you think, "Mart, I haven't got time for that...," or you find yourself rushing around one morning and speeding to work, just ponder on one question, which I think encapsulates them all:

"What makes me happy?"

This simple query is designed to ignite your introspection on what's going right in your life and what brings you that internal joy.

Spend a few minutes to express or write down everything that contributes to your happiness, no matter how small or grand. By focusing on these feelings of joy and gratitude, you set the stage for profound transformation, not only in your perception but in your overall well-being. When we feel good inside, it naturally extends outward, radiating positivity.

Recognising a Scarcity Mindset

Transitioning from a scarcity mindset, which focuses on what we lack, to an abundance mindset, which appreciates what we have, is quite a profound shift that can alter every aspect of our lives.

Gratitude is the bridge between these two states of mind.

A scarcity mindset often manifests as a persistent sense of not having enough, whether it's money, time, love or something else. It can lead to feelings of jealousy, insecurity and competition. Recognising these feelings and thought patterns is the first step in transforming them.

Reflect on the last week of your life and jot down any moments when you felt lacking or envious of others.

What triggered these feelings?

Understanding these triggers can help you begin to shift your focus.

Switching to an abundance mindset involves more than just positive thinking. It requires a deep-seated belief in the plentiful nature of the Universe. Gratitude plays a key role in fostering this belief by continually redirecting our focus from what we lack to what we possess.

Every time we express gratitude, we acknowledge the richness of our lives. Over time, this builds a psychological buffer against thoughts on scarcity and helps embed the belief that we live in a generous world.

Integrating gratitude into our daily routine can transform it from an occasional practice into a constant perspective. This habituation helps maintain the shift from scarcity to abundance, influencing our interactions, decisions and outlook.

Make it a habit to say "thank you" more often to others and to yourself.

Turn routine moments into opportunities for gratitude.

Making the shift from a scarcity to an abundance mindset through gratitude is transformative. This perspective change doesn't just make us happier; it makes us more open-hearted, resilient and connected. As we continue to cultivate gratitude, we find that abundance isn't something we achieve; it's something we tune into.

Pessimism vs. Optimism

Pessimism often involves focusing on the worst aspects of any situation, anticipating unfavourable outcomes, and generally having a gloomy view of the future. In contrast, optimism doesn't ignore challenges but approaches them with a mindset that looks for solutions and positive outcomes.

Gratitude acts as a buffer; regular expressions of gratitude can insulate our mindset against negativity. By appreciating what we have, we're less likely to spiral into despair when faced with difficulties. It helps us reframe challenges as opportunities for growth and learning, which is a core principle of optimism.

Numerous studies have demonstrated the psychological benefits of a grateful outlook. In fact, researchers recently found that participants who exercised gratitude for just a few weeks reported significantly better mental health just four weeks after compared to those who focused on negative or neutral experiences.[7]

One company even introduced a gratitude program where employees could acknowledge their peers' hard work and positive attributes.

Over six months, overall employee satisfaction and productivity significantly increased, demonstrating how gratitude can foster a positive workplace culture.

By consistently practising gratitude, we encourage an optimist's mindset, not only enhancing our emotional and mental well-being but also improving our physical health and interpersonal relationships. Seeing the glass as half full isn't about naivety, where you're ignoring life's pressures and pains; it's about choosing a life perspective that actively seeks out and celebrates the good despite the hardship. Gratitude empowers us to face the world with confidence, highlighting rays of hope during those tough times when all else seems dark.

Before starting my self-development and spiritual journey, I was a bit of a pessimist myself.

Something would go wrong, I'd beat myself up over it, something else negative would follow, and before I knew it, I'd be muttering the words, "Why me?" Because I couldn't believe all the bad luck I was having. I'd think to myself, "What have I got to be grateful for? Absolutely nothing!"

This is totally normal, as we all experience moments like this from time to time. It's really hard to activate that optimism inside ourselves when we're feeling like everything is constantly pitted against us.

Trust me when I tell you that gratitude works!

If you really struggle to think of anything to be grateful for, start with something super small, such as the fact that you have a roof over your head – many people don't.

Be grateful that you have running water – some countries don't.

Feel gratitude for having eyes to see or ears to hear. Think about what your life would be like if you didn't have those senses and how hard life might be for you.

Starting with the most fundamental aspects of our lives can often rekindle a sense of gratitude, especially on difficult days. Once you begin to appreciate the basics such as shelter, water or your senses, you can expand this gratitude to other often overlooked areas.

Be thankful for the variety of foods at your disposal, for the ability to taste a spectrum of flavours – some people have limitations that restrict their diets significantly.

Appreciate the bed you sleep in, the comfort of a warm blanket and the security of a lock on your door. Many live without these comforts.

Express gratitude for the ability to communicate, to express thoughts and emotions, to engage in conversations. Consider how vital this is to forming relationships and navigating your world.

Some people face challenges with communication, making every successful interaction they have even more precious.

Be grateful for your health if you are healthy and for the medical care available to you if you're not. Healthcare is a privilege that not everyone has easy access to.

Remember to be thankful for the people in your life, whether they're friends, family or even kind strangers you encounter. Relationships are a cornerstone of our well-being, and even those small, brief, positive interactions can have a profound impact on our day.

Gratitude can also extend to the experiences that have shaped you: the hard lessons, the victories, the quiet moments of reflection. Each one has contributed to the depth of your character and the breadth of your understanding.

Feel gratitude for nature; for the green grass under your feet, the trees that provide shade and the clouds that dance across the sky. These daily spectacles of nature are available to us all, but not everyone takes the time to notice and appreciate them.

Finally, be grateful for the time you have. Every minute is an opportunity to change, to grow, to experience and to live fully. Time is one resource we all have equally, yet it's easy to forget its value until it's scarce.

By anchoring your sense of gratitude in these foundational elements of life, you may find that your perception begins to shift. The more you practise gratitude, the more you realise there is so much to be grateful for, and this abundance mindset can truly transform your experience of life.

Scientists have proven that the brain houses what is called a "negativity bias," which means it seeks out, remembers and holds on to all of the tough and annoying things that happen in our day-to-day lives.[8] It glosses over the good things, and this is an evolutionary survival mechanism that we've learnt over time. Because of this, we forget the unexpected smiles and hugs from our children, the small moments of appreciation from friends and even all the lovely little snuggles we might get from our pets – all the stuff that we just take for granted in order to overcome the brain's tendency for negativity.

We need to cultivate a regular practice of soaking in the good stuff and feeding those small moments of joy and happiness and allowing them to take over our bodies, without feeling self-indulgent or guilty.

Regularly doing this enables us to become more robust and resilient human beings. I know that I feel happier and peaceful when I practise gratitude, and I also become a source of joy for other people, too.

In embracing gratitude as a continuous journey, you open yourself to a life that is continually enriched and enlivened by an awareness of and appreciation for the abundance around you. As you move forward, let gratitude be your compass, guiding your steps towards a more fulfilling, optimistic and interconnected life.

Gratitude acts as a magnet for manifesting our dreams. It aligns our energy with that of abundance and possibility, making us more receptive to opportunities and open to taking the steps necessary to achieve our goals. By appreciating what we already have, we open the door to more: more joy, more growth and more fulfilment. It teaches us that, often, the journey towards our dreams is as enriching as the destination itself, reminding us that every step, no matter how small, is a part of the beautiful path of our lives.

In this way, gratitude isn't just about being thankful for what we have, it's a powerful tool for creating the life that we envision!

Imagine if you approached the world each day with a heart so full of gratitude that it could see the hidden silver linings in every situation, no matter how small or ordinary. What if gratitude isn't just about being thankful for the good days but also about finding value in the challenges?

This transformative approach could turn every moment of despair into a stepping stone towards growth. Every setback and every disappointment becomes a moment ripe with potential, asking you to not just endure it but extract wisdom from it. By viewing life through this lens of gratitude, you're not just surviving. You're *thriving*, constantly accumulating emotional and spiritual wealth from every experience handed to you.

When gratitude becomes as natural as breathing, you begin to attract more of what resonates with that high vibrational energy. It's like turning on a light in the darkness – the brighter your light of gratitude, the more abundance flies to you like moths to a flame.

As you practise gratitude, watch as your life transforms, not because the world changes, but because your perception of it does.

I'll end this chapter with this one question, this one journal prompt, and this one thought-provoking statement:

"How will you change your life using gratitude?"

Activity

Think of a difficult situation you've recently faced in your life. This could be losing someone or something close to you, a grievance in your workplace or even something as small as missing the bus to work.

Write down at least three things this situation has taught you or how it's helped you grow.

Reflect on how recognising these aspects shifts your feelings about the situation.

This exercise is designed to transform our perspective on challenges, turning them from purely negative experiences into opportunities for personal growth and gratitude.

Chapter 6
Finding Tranquility Through Meditation and Mindfulness

I magine that you're snowed under with so much work that you've had to work overtime most evenings and weekends to just get caught up. This all adds extra pressure onto your relationships: Your family starts feeling like you've deserted them while your friends begin to think you're not making an effort for them. You end up in a bit of a flap, feeling overwhelmed, stressed and disconnected.

The more you try to manage and compartmentalise each aspect of your life, the more you miss out on important moments and milestones. Dinners at home, evenings with your children, weekend outings, and casual meet-ups with friends become rare occasions.

Yet the workload continues to pile up. The mental and emotional toll becomes palpable. Sleep becomes elusive as your mind races through endless to-do lists at night. You notice a persistent sense of fatigue clouding your days, your mood fluctuates more frequently, and your health starts to take a hit.

Anxiety begins to creep in, making it harder to concentrate and stay productive, which only perpetuates the cycle of stress and overflow of work.

In this state, your relationships suffer further.

Misunderstandings and frustrations grow as loved ones and friends might feel neglected or undervalued by your constant unavailability. Conversations may turn into confrontations, with you on the defensive justifying your absence in the lives of those who matter most. The guilt of letting down the people you care about adds another layer of stress to an already heavy load.

This scenario unfolds as a clear signal that something needs to change. That change runs from maintaining professional productivity to preserving personal well-being and relationships.

This moment of realisation is where the transformative potential of mindfulness and meditation becomes evident. By introducing these practices into your daily routine, you begin to create spaces of calm and reflection in your busy schedule, helping to manage stress and reconnect with what truly matters.

By choosing to step back and engage in a brief mindfulness practice, you begin to break the cycle of stress. This could be even just a few minutes of focused breathing or a mindful walk. This pause allows you to regain a sense of control over your reactions, helping you approach your workload and relationships with a clearer, more composed mindset.

Meditation, in this context, acts as a reset button, providing a much-needed refuge from the chaos of your busy life. It offers a space to clear your mind, reduce anxiety, and enhance your focus and productivity when you return to your tasks.

Meanwhile, maintaining a regular mindfulness practice helps cultivate a habit of presence, ensuring that you're more attuned to your needs and those of the people around you. As you continue practising, you'll find that you're not only more productive but also more connected and balanced, which naturally alleviates the pressure on your relationships and improves your overall well-being.

What Is Meditation?

I bet even just hearing the word "meditation" conjures up lots of images in your head of a monk, dressed in a robe, sat on the floor, legs crossed, chanting "aummm"!

I know that's exactly how I felt before I got into meditation. That might be why I put off doing it for so long. But meditation is far more diverse and accessible than these stereotypical images suggest. It doesn't require any special equipment, clothing, or environment. You can meditate anywhere – whether on a park bench, in your office chair, or in the quiet confines of your bedroom. The core of meditation isn't about how you look whilst doing it but about taming the mind and finding stillness within, which is a practice that can benefit everyone, irrespective of their lifestyle.

It's important to understand that meditation isn't bound to any specific culture or religion. While it's true that it has spiritual roots, the modern practice of meditation has evolved into a non-sectarian tool for enhancing mental health and well-being. This adaptation makes it inclusive and beneficial for people from all walks of life, regardless of their spiritual beliefs or background.

I worked in the mental health sector of the NHS for 15 years. I discovered meditation back in 2014. I was 27 at the time, and I'd often walk into my manager Karen's office to find her with her chair reclined, the lights dimmed, and her eyes closed. For about a year, I thought she just liked to have afternoon naps, if I'm totally honest! I had no idea that she was meditating until I asked if everything was OK at home – what with her sleeping at her desk daily – her face was a picture, as you can imagine!

She explained to me that, because of her heavy workload, sometimes the most productive thing she could do was meditate and connect with her breathing to bring stillness to her body and allow herself to arrive in the present moment.

I was shook!

Why had nobody told me about this before?

I started asking questions about the health benefits, how to get started, and how long it would take me to see results, and she kindly explained everything she knew about it. She even told me that, in the NHS Recovery College (a place where service users and carers broaden their knowledge of mental health conditions and well-being activities), they ran a four-week meditation course for staff. She didn't have to tell me twice; I swiftly joined.

If I'm honest with you, I found it quite an odd experience. It was all so new to me. I tried time and time again to quiet my mind and just be there in the present moment, but my mind was always flooded with thoughts like:

"I'm sat here meditating, and my email inbox is piling up."

"I wonder what I'm going to have for tea tonight?"

I just couldn't seem to switch off.

What I did notice, however, is that my anxious and depressive thoughts seemed to dissipate, as though by magic. It was at this point that I started questioning: Was this because of meditation?

Research shows that meditation can significantly reduce stress, anxiety, and depression. It enhances concentration, attention, and the ability to multitask[9]. Meditation also helps improve sleep and decrease blood pressure, and likewise aids in the management of pain and discomfort. These benefits aren't just subjective but are supported by an increasing number of scientific studies measuring changes in brain structure and function among regular meditators.

Anyone can do this, including you!

To start meditating, all you need is a few minutes each day. Here's a simple way to begin:

Find a quiet spot. Minimise distractions by finding a quiet place where you can relax.

Set a time limit. Start with just five minutes a day. As you get more comfortable with the practice, you can gradually increase this time.

Focus on your breath. Close your eyes and bring your attention to your breath. Breathe naturally, without trying to control your breath, and pay attention to the sensation of each inhale and exhale, following the air from your nostrils to down your throat, filling up your lungs, and back up and out of your mouth.

Notice when your mind wanders. It's natural for your mind to wander, just like mine did constantly. When you notice this happening, gently bring your attention back to your breath, which will centre you in the present moment.

Be kind to your wandering mind. Don't judge yourself or obsess over the content of the thoughts you find yourself lost in. Just come back to your breath over and over again, without criticism.

Incorporating meditation into your daily routine can be as simple as making it a habit to meditate at the same time each day. You can tie it to another daily activity like after brushing your teeth in the morning or right before bed. Consistency is key here, not just for cultivating discipline but for reaping the long-term benefits that meditation offers.

It's a versatile, powerful practice that anyone can use to foster mental clarity and emotional stability. By regularly practising meditation, you engage in a transformative process that can profoundly impact all areas of your life, leading to greater peace, balance, and fulfilment.

So why wait? Let go of any lingering misconceptions and dive into meditation.

You might just find that it's exactly what you needed all along!

Once I'd gotten to grips with meditation, I was doing it most mornings after waking. On days when I forgot to meditate, I took note that my day always somehow ended up chaotic, almost as though the meditation was keeping everything in check for me.

About two months had passed since I started on my meditation journey, and I noticed that Karen kept booking time out in her diary for something called "mindfulness." Back then, I had no clue what that was either.

But Karen was such a zen person; nothing ever seemed to phase her. One day after a stress-inducing meeting, I started to connect the dots. I asked her how she kept her cool, and she mentioned that she practised mindfulness. Obviously, I was massively intrigued and asked her what this was about, too.

Come to think of it, maybe Karen was sent to me for a reason to start me off on my spiritual journey! She was a fountain of knowledge not just in her role within the NHS but spiritually, too.

The description that she gave me of mindfulness has stuck with me for all these years.

She said, "Have you ever driven somewhere, and you've arrived at your destination without having any memory of how you got there, because you were too busy thinking about something else in your mind? Thinking about the future can cause anxiety, thinking about the past can cause depression, but being present in the current moment allows you to switch off from everything else and be still and at one with everything around us."

As you can imagine, my mind was blown!

When I asked her why it was in her diary every week, she mentioned that our employer offered weekly classes for staff. It was part of them looking after our well-being. In these classes, they allowed you to take time out of your working day to attend a group setting with other staff members to practise mindfulness.

Obviously, I jumped at the opportunity, so off I went to my 12-week mindfulness course.

I've got to admit, the first time I turned up at this class, there were about 14 of us in the room and our course leader, Jo, was like Princess Diana...if she had smoked weed! She was elegant and mysterious, but also so chill and relaxed – everything seemed to be happening at a snail's pace when she was around.

This frustrated me a little at first because I really wanted to wind her up and let her go. Anyone who knows me knows that I do everything at the speed of light, and I'm always going at 200mph, but I sharply learned that this may just be the reason why I was constantly burning myself out.

At the start of the course, Jo had us answer a questionnaire about our mood and mental health. This was so that we could see at the end of the 12 weeks whether the course had been beneficial for us. This is also a great practice if this is all new to you: Maybe you could write yourself a couple of paragraphs about your current mood and how you currently feel about all aspects of your life, and then review it in a month or two once you've practised mindfulness yourself to see if you too have an increase in mood.

The first exercise Jo had us all do was called a body scan, which involved us simply closing our eyes and checking in with our bodies.

This is a little exercise that we can all do right now, it'll only take a minute and I'll discuss the benefits of it straight after.

Mindfulness Body Scan

Sitting comfortably, close your eyes, and firstly notice your breathing. Notice how your chest rises and falls with every breath. Don't change your breathing pattern, just notice it, focusing all your attention on your breath.

Just as before, try to follow a full breath from your nose down to the back of your throat, inflating your lungs, and back up your throat and out of your mouth.

Notice which parts of your body are connected to the chair or seat you're sitting on:

What sensations do you feel from the gravity holding you to it?

How do your feet feel resting on the chair?

How does your back feel supporting your body upright?

Are there any niggles or pains?

If your mind wanders, don't worry about it – simply acknowledge that it has and bring your consciousness back to the present moment of you sitting upright.

Notice your mood. Are you happy? Sad? Exhausted? Hyper?

Connect with your self-awareness and self-compassion, allowing yourself to acknowledge these feelings. Be curious and ask yourself why you feel this mood right now in this present moment. Once you're ready to, you can open your eyes again.

You just practised mindfulness and meditated in the process of doing so! Although that was a brief exercise, you can see that this is what mindfulness and meditation are all about: being present in the current moment.

I like to do this little exercise every single day. I do it two to three times even on extremely stressful days if I remember to. It only takes a brief minute, but it's extremely effective for managing stress, anxiety and depression.

Let's say for example that you're at work. You have a bit of a disagreement with a colleague and suddenly feel angry. Your mind then goes into overdrive, and you start thinking about what just happened and all of the things you could have said. You then start ruminating about the future and how the atmosphere is going to be especially awkward in the coming days....

STOP!

Mindfulness will bring you back to the present moment and stop your mind from going into overdrive. It allows you to process what's going on in that moment rather than what could have been or what will be.

Mindfulness is well-known for its ability to reduce stress. It helps by enabling us to respond to stressful situations with awareness of our reactions rather than reacting automatically. This mindful approach can lower our cortisol levels, the hormone associated with stress.

Practising mindfulness daily helps us gain control over our emotions by increasing our awareness and acceptance of emotional states without judgement. This can lead to more stable and measured responses to emotional stimuli. It also exercises the brain's ability to focus on the present moment, which can enhance overall cognitive function, increase attention spans and reduce mind-wandering and distractions, which I'm sure you can all relate to from time to time!

Numerous studies have shown that mindfulness meditation can significantly decrease symptoms of anxiety and depression[10]. It helps by altering thought patterns and reducing rumination and negative thinking, which are common triggers of anxiety and depressive episodes. By calming the mind and reducing stress, mindfulness can lead to improved sleep patterns. It helps us to fall asleep faster and stay asleep longer by mitigating the racing thoughts often associated with sleep disturbances.

Mindfulness is even effective in managing chronic pain. It doesn't necessarily reduce the sensation of pain, but it changes the way we perceive and respond to pain, which can diminish our suffering.

Regular mindfulness practice can contribute to cardiovascular health by reducing blood pressure. This reduction is believed to be the result of enhanced relaxation and stress management. It can even foster an improved body image and greater self-esteem. By promoting acceptance and reducing judgement towards ourselves, mindfulness can enhance overall well-being and body satisfaction.

The reason why most people practise it overall, however, is that it helps build resilience by promoting flexibility in thinking and the ability to handle unexpected challenges. Mindful individuals are better able to adapt to new situations with less anxiety and stress.

These benefits demonstrate why mindfulness has become a cornerstone technique in contemporary psychological practices aimed at improving mental health and the overall quality of life. Whether practised through formal meditation, integrated into daily activities or applied in therapeutic settings, mindfulness offers tools for a healthier, more focused and emotionally balanced life.

Mindful Walking

Some of the other exercises Jo had us do seemed a little odd at the time – almost to the point that I started questioning my own sanity. There were days when I just thought, "What on earth are we doing?"

One activity we did was called mindful walking. It's also something you can do next time you nip out anywhere, as you walk your dog or on your walk to work, when you're out with the kids, and so on. This activity is just to get you to notice things.

Noticing how your feet feel as they hit the ground with each step you take. Using your senses, what can you see, hear, smell and touch around you?

Even if you practise this for just five minutes out of your walk, you're bringing your mind to the present moment rather than letting it wander. Your mood should improve because you aren't allowing your mind time to become anxious or worried about other situations going on in your life.

I do this most days on my dog walks – we have a little Jack Russell called JJ, and whenever we go out for a walk, I like to take my surroundings in and notice the leaves on the trees or the blades of grass blowing in the wind down to the stony gravel on the path. I try to take in all of my surroundings where usually I would have just walked by without noticing. It really does work wonders for the mind.

It was pouring the day we first did mindful walking with Jo. So, she asked us to move all the chairs to the outside of the room and told us that we were just going to do this exercise indoors. We all proceeded to take our shoes and socks off and started walking around the room slowly, feeling the ground underneath our feet. We were all doing this in silence to give it our full attention.

To anyone observing us through the window, we must have looked like mindless zombies. There were a few moments where I would make eye contact with someone else in the class and we would start giggling, too, because it felt so unnatural and odd.

But mindful walking has changed how I now go out and explore the world. I used to walk along, head on my phone, bumping into people. Then I'd suddenly look up and wonder how I'd walked so far because I hadn't paid any attention to the journey. Now, I practise mindful walking most lunch times, just to get out and stretch my legs and take my mind off things that have built up work-wise over the morning.

Mindful Eating

Another form of mindfulness we looked at in my course was mindful eating. We were all given a raisin to hold in our hands. We then had five minutes to look at this raisin – yes, really! – and pass it between our fingers and notice how it felt and looked and smelt like and even put it in our mouth but not chew it. It was after the five minutes that we were finally allowed to eat it.

We must have looked like camels rolling this tiny raisin around in our mouths, but once we ate it, the flavours tasted vastly different than just scoffing one random raisin. The opposite is like if you had made yourself some food, sat down in front of the TV and watched a film. You'd get so invested in the film that your mind would be elsewhere; you wouldn't be taking in those flavours and smells of your food. We all do it. For the majority of the time, we mindlessly eat our food without any thought, not actually taking in any of its flavours.

But by being fully present as the raisin exercise proved to show, you've allowed yourself to really concentrate on what you're eating. Moreover, this has been medically proven to reduce overeating in adults[11]. Slowing down and taking your time whilst eating helps your brain realise more quickly that you're full. This in turn teaches you not to overindulge just for the sake of eating.

Try this next time you have some food and see what you notice. It's not for everyone, but doing so does take your mind off other things and keep you present.

Over the next week or so after reading this, give mindfulness a try for yourself. If you find that you don't like it, you don't have to continue. The core principle of both meditation and mindfulness is all about allowing yourself to try something new and having compassion for yourself if you realise it's not for you.

Speaking from experience, it has really helped me stop worrying about what happened in the past and what's to come in the future, which allows me to focus my time and energy on the here and now.

Once you've practised meditation or mindfulness for a while, go back to those initial couple of paragraphs you wrote at the beginning of this chapter and ask yourself how your mood and feelings have changed since then.

Have they improved?

Do you feel like you have more clarity and understanding in your life?

Are your anxious thoughts still harbouring your mind like before?

If there are any signs of improvement, they would be a great indicator for you to stick to it and carry on with this practice.

Since incorporating mindfulness and meditation into my daily life, I've gained enhanced clarity in my general well-being and a better appreciation for moment-to-moment experiences. These practices have allowed me to respond to life's challenges with a greater sense of calm and purpose rather than reacting impulsively. It's as if I've developed a mental buffer that cushions the stress and chaos that used to overwhelm me.

This clarity has also improved my decision-making processes, making me more attentive to my needs and the needs of others. As a result, relationships feel richer, work feels more manageable, and daily stresses feel less daunting.

This overall improvement in mental and emotional health has been a transformative experience, underscoring the tangible benefits that mindfulness and meditation can bring to our lives.

There are some amazing apps out there such as Headspace or Calm that guide you through mindful practices you can do. You can even head to my YouTube channel or Insight Timer profile, where you'll find free guided mindfulness and meditation videos that are quick and easy to complete in under 10 minutes.

I truly believe in the tranquillity, peace, and calm that these exercises bring into my life, and I'm so grateful for having discovered them many years ago and allowing myself to practise their teachings daily.

Meditation and mindfulness can alter the surface of your thoughts. With every session, the tumultuous waves of stress and anxiety die down until your mind becomes like a serene lake, its surface smooth and undisturbed, perfectly mirroring the sky above and reflecting a clearer version of the world and yourself.

With each mindful step and conscious breath, you enrich your existence, transforming everyday life into something not just bearable but deeply satisfying.

Activity

To support your journey towards greater mindfulness and inner peace, I've created a guided mindfulness audio, which you can freely download at cannycrystalsacademy.co.uk/limitless.

This audio is specially tailored, and designed to lead you through a series of calming, focused exercises that will help ground your thoughts, centre your emotions and enhance your overall awareness of the present moment.

This guided mindfulness session serves as a practical tool to introduce you to the practice of mindfulness or deepen your existing practice. The audio guides you step-by-step through breathing techniques and mental imagery that promote relaxation and concentration. To make the most of this resource, find a quiet place where you can sit or lie down comfortably without interruptions. Use headphones to fully immerse yourself in the experience and try to dedicate this time solely to your mindfulness practice.

I recommend listening to this guided audio daily, ideally at a consistent time, such as in the morning to start your day centred or in the evening to unwind and clear your mind before sleep. Regular practice can significantly enhance your mental clarity, reduce stress, and improve your emotional resilience. Let this guided mindfulness audio be your daily retreat, helping you to cultivate a tranquil mind and a serene outlook on life.

Chapter 7

Integrating Crystals Into Your Daily Life

I magine you're navigating through a dense forest thick with undergrowth and obscured pathways. Every step forward feels uncertain and fraught with obstacles. The trees are so closely packed that sunlight barely touches the forest floor, and the air feels stagnant and heavy, pressing down on you with every breath. As you push forward, the sense of direction becomes increasingly muddled and the forest seems endless. You start to feel disoriented, lost with no one to guide you.

This is exactly how I felt back in 2019 when I felt like the whole world was always out to get me. The forest is much like the complicated landscape of our daily lives, filled as they are with stress, obligations and the constant buzz of activity. Just as the dense trees block out the light, our commitments and worries cloud our perspective, making it hard to find our way. The paths we take are not only physically taxing but also emotionally draining, leaving within us a longing for a clearing, a place for respite.

Now, imagine finding a compass, and, unlike a traditional compass, this one doesn't point North. Instead, it guides you toward internal balance and focus.

Each crystal, from the calming energies of amethyst to the joyous properties of citrine, offers a unique form of guidance, clearing the mental fog and illuminating your path with its own inherent personality.

Just as the right tools can help you navigate through a physical forest, these crystals can be your compass, providing the clarity and support needed to manage life's complexities.

When I started using crystals for myself, the forest didn't seem so impenetrable anymore. The air felt lighter, the paths became clearer and what once felt like concrete obstacles now appeared as manageable challenges. It was as though sunlight had started to break through the leaves, casting gentle, shimmering rays that guided me along my journey. My sense of direction was restored and with each step, I felt more grounded and centred.

The crystals didn't change the forest. They changed how I moved through it, turning my disorienting trek into an empowered journey.

When I was first introduced to crystals, I remember thinking, "How is this little rock going to do anything for me at all?" – I just couldn't see the energy or the power behind them. But how wrong I was. They changed my entire life in an instant.

Crystal Healing

We all know by now that everything is energy. Everything has a makeup of energy in some way shape or form. Crystals act as a power hold for healing – like a battery, if you'd like to think of it that way – as they allow positive and exciting energy to flow into the body and do away with the negative, toxic energy. They work by channelling your energy levels and focusing on healing your body from the inside out.

It was once solely thought that crystals just carried the power to induce the placebo effect in the body, which is scientifically proven to help medical treatment.[12] But crystals have their own particular vibration and frequency, which arise from their unique molecular composition. From the way they move and interact, these vibrations and energies work in benefiting and uplifting our mood, mind and health in a considerable manner, similar to the way that essential oils and aromatherapy work. We'd all be pretty open to going for an aromatherapy massage if we had the chance, wouldn't we?

So why is crystal healing any different?

Much like how aromatherapy harnesses the subtle powers of essential oils to enhance well-being through our sense of smell, crystal healing utilises the natural energies of crystals to promote balance and healing in our physical, emotional and spiritual bodies. The scepticism often arises from crystal healing's less tangible mode of action, which, unlike aromatherapy's more immediately noticeable effects through scent, works on an energetic level that some may find harder to grasp or directly feel.

However, when you consider that everything in the Universe vibrates at specific frequencies, including ourselves, the concept of crystals affecting our energies doesn't seem so far-fetched.

When placed in our environment or used in practices such as meditation or body layouts, these crystals can help harmonise our own energies with the natural order of the Earth, leading to an improved mood, mental clarity and overall health.

Since they're all naturally extracted from the Earth, crystals harness the healing energies of the Sun, Moon and oceans to improve our energetic state.

When you place or hold a crystal over the body, it interacts with the body's chakras and promotes physical and mental wellness. If you use them in a certain way, they can even improve your concentration and creativity and promote physical, emotional and spiritual cleansing.

Crystals vibrate at the same pitch as humans and maximise the healing abilities we already have, uplifting the positive energy deep within us. This is also the same reason for the comforting feeling a crystal generates when placed on your body; you connect with it better and feel more at ease.

They've become so much less of a taboo subject as of late, and people are much more willing these days to give crystal healing a shot. I often say to people: "It's not harming anyone – what have you got to lose?"

Crystals have been used for centuries for healing, protection and manifestation. Each crystal has a unique vibrational energy that can align with ours, amplifying our desires and supporting their manifestation into the physical realm.

To put it as simply as I can, every crystal possesses a unique internal structure, and that allows it to resonate at a certain frequency. This is why different crystals are believed to have different effects on our emotional, physical and energetic health.

For instance, clear quartz is known for its high vibrational frequency, making it a master healer and a powerful crystal for manifesting any intention. On the other hand, we have rose quartz, which vibrates at a frequency of love and harmony, and that's going to be ideal for attracting self-love and nurturing our relationships.

When we consciously work with these vibrations, we can choose crystals that align with our specific goals and intentions, and that will enhance our manifestation efforts.

Maybe you struggle with attracting wealth, or love, or success, or happiness...trust me when I say, there's a crystal for everything.

Choosing Your Crystal

The key is to select crystals that resonate with you personally and your desires.

I often get messages from people saying, "Which crystal would you suggest for me?" My answer is the same each time.

Although I can give you a recommendation, it's ultimately about what resonates with you and what you want in life.

You could ask yourself open-ended questions like:

"What do I want most in life?"

"What is my body calling out for?"

"If I had a magic wand, what one thing would I change?"

These questions will help you tap into your deepest needs and desires, guiding you toward choosing crystals that align best with your personal journey and aspirations. By reflecting on these questions, you're not just picking out a crystal for its physical beauty or popular attributes. You're searching for a crystal that will serve as a partner in your spiritual and emotional growth. This introspective approach ensures that the crystals you select are more than just decorative items; they become tools of empowerment!

Once you have clarity on what you seek or need to change, matching those intentions with specific crystals can amplify their effectiveness. For instance, if you crave more calmness and stability in your life, a crystal like blue lace agate or lepidolite could be ideal for you. Conversely, if you're seeking energy and courage to tackle new challenges, carnelian or red jasper might resonate more.

The connection you feel with a crystal is just as important as its purported properties. The resonance you experience when holding a crystal in your hands, the attraction you feel towards its colour or shape, or the calmness it might instil within you are all signs that it's the right choice for you. Trust your instincts and let your intuition guide you in selecting the right crystals. This intuitive connection ensures that the energy you invest in and receive from these crystals is both meaningful and transformative, in turn enhancing your journey towards personal fulfilment and well-being.

Cleansing Your Crystal

I like to think of crystals as sponges, absorbing all negativity from those they come into contact with. The mines I work with dig these crystals from the ground. They then buffer them, shape them, cut them and then post them out to me. My team and I then pack them up and send them to you. Those crystals will have absorbed some of my energy and intentions and those of the people who dug them from the ground down to some of the person who delivered them through your letterbox. Therefore, before you begin working with your crystals, it's essential to cleanse and charge them.

Cleansing removes any previous energy the crystal has absorbed, ensuring it's attuned to your energy. There are several methods to cleanse crystals such as running them under natural water from a stream or a river or even the sea.

When myself and Fran went on that cruise in 2023, for example, we had a beach day in the south of France. I took a handful of crystals in my bum-bag down to the sea and washed them all in the beautifully crisp and refreshing water. I love anything like that; it feels so aligned for me – I feel like it's almost the Earth giving them a little kiss and a boost of energy.

There are other ways of cleansing, too. You can smudge with sage or incense, letting the smoke wash away their negativities, use a sound bowl and allow the vibrations gently dissolve any impurities, or the most popular way, place them in moonlight or sunlight for their energies to cleanse and revitalise your crystal.

There are so many ways to cleanse, just ensure you do your due diligence to see if your method is suitable for that specific crystal – a quick Google search would advise you instantly. For example, if you put something like selenite in water, it would eventually dissolve.

I would know. When I first started getting into crystals, I remember treating myself to a huge ruby aura quartz tower. When it arrived, I instantly fell in love with it and thought, "This would be the perfect crystal to meditate with in the bath this afternoon." So, off I went to run a steaming, hot bath. I popped the ruby aura quartz in the water with me, laid down to soak, closed my eyes and started to meditate.

Roughly 15 minutes had passed before I opened my eyes to what can only be described as a blood bath! The water was bright red, swirling around me and my first thought was to jump up, thinking I was bleeding to death!

So, there I was, stood totally naked in my bathroom in shock, and as I looked at my skin, it almost looked metallic! I fished my crystal out of the water. To my surprise, it was now clear instead of that beautiful red hue.

I remember messaging Carly, who I'd bought it from, that it must have been a fake because I was standing there with red-stained, shimmering skin and she instantly sent me a voice note back laughing her head off at me.

Nobody told me that aura-coated crystals are quartz that undergo a process in which the surface is bonded with vaporised or atomised metals like gold, platinum or titanium. This process creates a thin layer or coating on the crystal, resulting in a colourful iridescence and a metallic sheen that enhances the crystal's appearance.

Well, that thin coating had come away and was now swirling around the plughole, heading down the drain.

In all fairness, I should have done my research before purchasing and although I see the funny side now, I was mortified at the time! I still have the clear quartz crystal in my bathroom to this day, because it's a reminder for me to think about what I'm putting in the bath with me!

The larger lesson is that crystals are just like anything else. You have to put in some form of work to get the most out of them. When it comes to placing crystals, some people store them on shelves around their houses, some keep them in a bowl and some even keep them in their bras to always be around their energy.

Personally, though, I don't think you can just leave them to sit on a shelf in your house and expect them to work, day in, day out, for all eternity.

But that's what most people do, and then they pass crystal healing off, as they've tried it, and it didn't work for them.

As I mentioned earlier, we have to look at crystals as though they're batteries. Sooner or later they're going to need charging!

If you left your mobile phone for a month on a shelf, do you really think you're still going to be receiving calls and texts?

No! You're going to need to give it a bit of love and stick it on charge!

As a general rule of thumb, I go around the house once a week or so playing a Tibetan singing bowl or with an incense stick, blowing smoke across my crystals, just to refresh the energy of the crystals and give them a boost of life.

After reading this chapter, I want you to select a crystal that you feel drawn to or that aligns with a current goal or desire that you have. If you're new to crystals, clear quartz would be a versatile starting point.

Once chosen, cleanse your crystal using one of the methods I mentioned, but, quite honestly, feel free to experiment. Use your intuition to guide you to the best cleansing method for you and your crystal.

After cleansing it, reflect on the connection you've started forming with your crystal. How does it feel in your presence?

Imagine the possibilities as you continue to explore and deepen that relationship. It's almost like getting into the mindset of seeing the crystal as one of your friends.

You've got to give it a little love and attention every once in a while, or you might as well not have it at all.

Setting Intentions

Having introduced ourselves to the crystal we want to work with, it's time to dive deeper by focusing on how to align their energies with our deepest intentions.

Intentions act as the seed of our desires. When combined with the crystals' potent power, a fertile ground for our dreams to take root and flourish. There's a symbiotic relationship between crystal energy and our intentions. By learning to harness this connection, we can manifest our wildest goals.

After cleansing, I'll sit with my crystals in my hands and for just a few moments I like to close my eyes, visualise with them and sometimes even speak to them, telling them what I want them to help me with in my life. This is classed as setting your intentions.

It could even be something as simple as saying, "Come on then – show me how good today can get!"

I think there's something so powerful about speaking your intentions to your crystals and letting them know where you want help in your life. Yes, you might look like a nut-job whilst doing it, but honestly, it really works!

The process of aligning your crystal with your intention begins with clear, focused thought. It's crucial to articulate your intention with as much specificity and positivity as possible. This isn't merely about wishing; it's about setting a clear direction for your energy and the crystal's energy to flow.

To effectively program your crystal with your intention, hold the crystal in your hands, close your eyes and take deep, slow breaths to centre yourself, just as you would any other time at the start of a meditation. Visualise your intention as a beam of light or a specific scene unfolding in your mind that represents your goal being achieved.

Feel the emotions tied to that visualisation as vividly as possible.

My three favourite emotions that I feel supercharge my crystal's intentions are feelings of joy, gratitude and peace, because these are high vibrations.

Then, speak your intention aloud or silently affirm it in your mind, imagining the energy of your words infusing the crystal and enveloping it from within.

It's that simple. You've now set your intentions!

Crystal Grids

Another way you can amplify crystal energy is by utilising a crystal grid.

A crystal grid is an arrangement of crystals that combines their energies to support a common goal. The collective energy of a crystal grid is more potent than using a single crystal because it amplifies the intention it's set for. You can buy crystal grid boards off Amazon. They're usually made up of geometric patterns upon which you can place your crystal at every point. You can even just Google one and print a picture of it.

In fact, the one I have on my desk at work is just a printed bit of paper with a crystal grid on it and, at the bottom, I've got a little affirmation written on it.

To create a simple manifestation grid, select a central crystal that represents your main intention and surround it with supporting crystals that align with your goal.

The one in my office is all about attracting financial wealth. At the centre of it, I have a large pyrite for cash flow, luck and prosperity. Surrounding that, I have citrine-tumbled stones for abundance and wealth. Finally, on the outside layer, I have lots of tiger's eye crystal chips for determination, focus and willpower to make this manifestation happen.

The arrangement doesn't have to be complex; it can be as simple as placing your central crystal on a piece of paper and surrounding it with smaller crystals in a circle. Don't overcomplicate this for yourself.

As you place each crystal, reaffirm your intention, envisioning the grid acting as a beacon, drawing your desire into reality. You can activate the grid by tracing an imaginary line between the crystals with your finger or a crystal point, visualising your intention flowing through the grid.

Feel free to use any additional crystals that support your intention, even if it's just one or two more.

As you arrange your grid, maintain a clear focus on your goal, pouring your intention into each crystal.

Once completed, spend a few moments each day sitting with your grid, because that will be reinvigorating your intention to manifest that desire.

Incorporating Crystals Into Our Daily Lives

Daily and in everything I do, I manage to incorporate crystals in some way, shape or form.

If I go in the bath, I have crystals for relaxation all around me like amethyst, howlite, celestite. On my desk at work, I have crystals to increase my productivity and creativity like clear quartz, aquamarine, and carnelian. In my car, I have highly grounding and protective crystals like tourmaline, black jasper and black obsidian, so I can drive around knowing I'm protected from everything else.

Just imagine what my house is like!

I've stationed many prosperity and abundance-boosting crystals, such as pyrite and citrine, in the wealth corner of my home following the Feng Shui *bagua*. I've got selenite to cleanse above my front door and labradorite behind the front door to transmute any negative energy into positivity. I have tiger's eye and rose quartz crystals in my relationship corner. I've got a giant lump of amethyst on my bedside table to help me have a rested night's sleep...

In fact, I don't think there's a room in my house that has less than two crystals in it – even my toilets!

The magic of crystals doesn't end with specific rituals or setups. Their true power shines when they become a part of our everyday existence, as they're constantly vibrating with the intentions we've imbued them with.

Crystals can accompany you in many forms throughout the day, each serving a unique purpose in your manifestation journey. Carrying a crystal in your pocket or purse ensures that its vibrational energy remains within your personal energy field, subtly influencing your thoughts, emotions and experiences towards your intentions.

Wearing crystals as jewellery keeps them close and serves as a constant reminder of your goals, doubling as a tool for focus and a statement of your commitment to your manifestations.

Placing crystals in your living or workspace creates an environment that supports your intentions, too. The key is to place these crystals where they can best support your daily activities and align with your manifestation goals.

Incorporating crystals into your meditation practice can profoundly deepen your connection to your intentions. Holding a crystal or placing it in front of you during meditation helps focus your mind and amplify your intentions, creating a powerful conduit for manifestational energy.

Focus on the sensation of the crystal in your hand or its visual appearance, allowing its energy to merge with yours. Visualise your intentions flowing into the crystal and out into the Universe, reinforced by the crystal's vibrational support.

A daily meditation, even for just a few short minutes, with your chosen crystal can significantly accelerate your manifestation process by keeping your intentions clear and your vibrational energy aligned.

To incorporate them into your life, reflect on the areas of your life you're focusing your manifestation efforts on. Choose a crystal that aligns with this intention for daily carry or wear. If your goal is more broad and general, such as overall well-being or balance, again, a clear quartz or selenite may be perfect due to its versatile, amplifying properties.

Consciously carry this crystal with you or, if you prefer, place it in a significant spot in your home or workspace. Throughout the day, whenever you notice the crystal, just pause to reaffirm your intention, letting this act as an anchor to realign you with your goals.

Integrating crystals into your daily life goes beyond carrying a piece of the Earth with you. You're enveloping yourself in a constant reminder of your intentions and the manifestation journey you're on. These practices will help maintain the momentum of your desires, ensuring that every moment is an opportunity for you to align with your goals.

Overcoming Obstacles Using Crystals

Crystals can be powerful allies in clearing the path toward your goals. Obstacles, whether internal like self-doubt and fear, or external, such as environmental stressors, can really have an impact on our progress. Crystals can help us overcome these hurdles, providing protection, clarity and the courage to move forward.

Our first step is to identify the obstacles currently standing in your way.

Reflect on what's been holding you back. Is it a lack of confidence, clarity or maybe even external negativity?

Once we pinpoint these challenges, we can match them with corresponding crystals.

For example, black tourmaline is excellent for shielding against negative energies, whilst tiger's eye can bolster confidence and reduce that internalised fear.

Protecting your energy field is crucial when navigating obstacles. Crystals can serve as a barrier against negativity and as a source of strength.

Creating a protective shield involves placing specific crystals around your home or workspace, carrying them with you, or even meditating with them.

Smoky quartz, for instance, is known for its ability to ground and protect, helping to dissipate emotional and environmental stress.

Activity

Select a crystal that resonates with the obstacle you wish to overcome.

Find a quiet space where you can sit comfortably.

Hold the crystal in your hand or place it in front of you.

Close your eyes, take deep breaths and visualise the obstacle in your path.

Imagine the crystal's energy enveloping this obstacle, dissolving it and transforming it into light.

Feel the obstacle losing its power over you, replaced by a sense of peace and confidence.

Conclude the meditation by visualising your path clear and open with your goal in sight.

Enhancing Intuition

Intuition acts as our internal compass, guiding us through decisions and insights that align closely with our soul's purpose. By strengthening our intuitive connection, we're better equipped to make choices that resonate with our deepest intentions and navigate our manifestation journey with greater clarity and confidence.

Various crystals are celebrated for their ability to open and enhance the third eye and crown chakras, which are the energy centres associated with intuition and spiritual connection. Lapis lazuli, with its deep blue colouring, can stimulate the third eye, enhancing insight and clarity in decision-making.

Incorporating crystals into your daily life or meditation practice can help attune your mind to the subtle whispers of your intuition, offering guidance and perspective aligned with your highest good.

You could even try choosing crystals intuitively. That's a practice that not only strengthens your connection with your crystals but also with your own inner guidance.

To practise intuitive selection, clear your mind and focus on your intention or a question you seek guidance on. Then, without overthinking, allow yourself to be drawn to a crystal, whether by its colour, shape or simply a feeling it evokes.

I often start my day by holding my hands over my huge collection in my spare room and just asking myself "What do I need to work with today?"

Trusting that intuitive choice fosters a deeper, more personal connection with your crystal and enhances its effectiveness in your manifestation work. This process can be repeated whenever you feel drawn to work with a new crystal or seek guidance on different aspects of your life as well. You can do it as many times a day as you like.

Activity

Choose a crystal intuitively.

Find a quiet space where you can sit comfortably without distractions.

Hold your crystal in your hand or place it in front of you, then close your eyes.

Take deep, slow breaths to centre yourself, and with each exhale, release any tension or clutter from your mind.

Visualise that crystal's energy almost forming a bubble around you, a gentle, vibrant light that opens your third eye and crown chakras.

Ask for clarity, insight or guidance on a specific issue or your manifestation journey in general.

Sit in this space, staying open and receptive for several minutes.

Afterwards, jot down any impressions, thoughts or feelings that arose during the meditation in a journal.

These insights are messages from your intuition, amplified through your crystal.

Manifesting with Crystals

Rituals are a potent way to focus your intention, energy and actions towards manifesting your desires. They create a sacred space for your intentions to be nurtured and allow for a deeper connection with the Universe's energy. You can create and craft personalised crystal rituals that harness the unique vibrational properties of crystals to support and amplify your manifestation efforts.

A crystal ritual involves intention, symbolism and the deliberate use of energy. The first step is to clearly define your intention. Think about what specific desire or goal you're focusing on. Next, ensure you choose crystals that resonate with this intention based on their properties.

The environment you choose to conduct your ritual in is also crucial. A quiet, comfortable space where you feel safe and undisturbed enhances the ritual's effectiveness. Incorporating elements like candles, incense or symbolic items that resonate with your intention can further amplify the energy of your ritual.

The lunar cycle also plays a significant role in manifestation, with the new moon and full moon phases offering particularly potent energies for beginning new projects and releasing what no longer serves us. A new moon ritual might involve setting intentions for what you wish to manifest in the coming cycle, using crystals like black moonstone or labradorite to seed these new beginnings.

A full moon ritual, on the other hand, can focus on releasing and cleansing. Here, you might use crystals like selenite or clear quartz to help clear any obstacles or old patterns hindering your manifestation path. Placing your crystals under the moonlight not only charges them with lunar energy but also symbolises the infusion of your intentions with the universe's abundant energies.

The Relationship with Your Crystal

Everything I've spoken about in this chapter is perfect for any beginner, or even those who have crystals but don't actively work with them. The relationship you cultivate with your crystals is unique and powerful, offering continuous support, guidance and vibrational alignment with your intentions.

So how do we now nurture that relationship, ensuring your crystal practice remains vibrant and effective?

Your crystals are more than just tools. Like I said before, you have to see them as your friends in your manifestation work. Caring for them is essential to keep their energy clear and potent. The care you invest in your crystals reflects the care you invest in your own energetic health and alignment.

Take a moment to reflect on this information when you get a chance.

What shifts have you noticed in your energy, your awareness or your manifestation journey since introducing crystals into your practice?

Reflecting on your experiences helps solidify your learning and growth, providing insights into how best to continue integrating crystals into your life.

Consider journaling about your crystal journey, noting any significant moments, insights or changes you experience. This not only serves as a record of your progress but can also highlight future paths for exploration and growth within your crystal practice.

Looking forward, consider how you'll continue to incorporate crystals into your daily life and manifestation work. Perhaps you'll set a routine for regular crystal meditations or maybe you're inspired to learn more about different crystals and their properties.

With all this in mind, set one small, achievable goal for your continued crystal practice.

Commit yourself.

It could be as simple as meditating with a crystal once a week, carrying a crystal daily for a month or even creating a new crystal grid for your home.

Write this goal down and place it somewhere visible as a reminder of your commitment to your growth and manifestation journey.

Moldavite

If I had a pound for every time I get asked about moldavite in a message, I'd be a millionaire, so I feel like I need to talk about this here.

For those out there who really want to supercharge their manifestations in all aspects of their lives, there's a tektite called moldavite, which was formed from the impact of a meteor that hit Earth over 15,000 years ago. Because of its highly transformational energies and the fact that it's highly rare, its price has shot through the roof in recent years.

I have a small piece on a necklace that I wear daily, which cost me about £75, and when I say small, I mean it's tiny – but I really do believe in the transformational power it brings to me daily.

Personally, I don't think it's scary, although a lot of you reading this right now will seem to think otherwise. I think the main reason that people are worried about working with it is all because of a TikTok video that went viral back in 2021.

A girl was proclaiming, "Don't buy this crystal, it will ruin your life." Trust me when I say this: No crystal gives off bad energy, they simply imbue and enhance the energy we already store within.

This girl claimed that, within a month of working with Moldavite, she lost her job. Next, her boyfriend broke up with her, so she had to move out of the home she had with him. She was now at rock bottom.

Just a month later, however, she put another video on the social media platform, which didn't go viral, ironically. The video described how she was since hired for the job of her dreams on almost double her salary; that she was so glad her boyfriend had ended their relationship as she found out he had been cheating on her and she was left a hefty lump sum in inheritance from her grandfather's death earlier that year to enable her to try and get a mortgage on her dream home.

But the damage was already done from that first video.

The first video had something ridiculous like 9 million views, the second had just 100 thousand.

Yes, it's going to be an intense ride, because Moldavite is known for its time-accelerating properties, and so what might have taken you years to notice, come to terms with and benefit from all happens to you within just a few short weeks.

I don't want to say it's the ultimate fertility crystal either, but, at the time of writing this, we're onto our 23rd Canny Crystals baby from customers who have worked with moldavite and since fallen pregnant... just putting that out there as a caveat. Be careful ladies!

The change it has made in my life has been astronomical. It's mad to think that, back in 2022, I was still working in the NHS in my usual nine to five, and running Canny Crystals in whatever spare time I had.

Now, I have my own office here on the Quayside in Newcastle. I turn over multiple six figures – which, to put this into context, is more in just one month than I was earning in an entire year working for the NHS!

When I told my family I was leaving the NHS, I was met with things like, "You can't leave the NHS to sell rocks," from my nanna, or "Martin, you've got a mortgage to pay, remember?" from my mam. And I get it, we came from nothing. No money at all. But all of this was them laying their fears and concerns out.

When I started working daily with my moldavite, I would receive little downloads of ideas from the Universe.

One day in 2022, I was meditating with my moldavite and had an idea pop into my head to message Fran from Law of Attraction Changed My Life and just ask outright to be on her podcast. At the time, she had the number 1 podcast for self-improvement in the UK, and we had messaged a couple of times prior to this – she seemed pretty friendly, so I just went for it, chewed the frog and took that inspired action.

Two weeks later and there I am, driving to her house in Lincoln – we recorded an episode of her podcast, an episode of my podcast, and what happened next was crazy!

On the following Friday, when both episodes came out, I remember waking up to over 100 orders, and immediately thought, "Oh my God – it's 7am, what the hell?"

That month, I hit my first £30k month and things haven't reverted since then. I thank Fran all the time for this, because it truly changed my business and she helped me grow.

Little nuggets of inspirational ideas and energy come from my Moldavite daily, and so I take it everywhere with me.

I nearly had a fit when it was almost confiscated at the airport on holiday in Malaga. I couldn't speak Spanish to tell the security that it was a "crystal" and instead, somehow told her it was "crystal meth." Thanks, Google Translate!

Moldavite isn't for everyone though, and I get that.

Choosing the right crystal is a personal journey. It's about what resonates with you and aligns with your life's desires. Reflect on what you seek to change or enhance in your life, and let these insights guide you toward crystals that will be most beneficial. Engaging with crystals in this way turns them from mere objects into companions in your spiritual and emotional growth.

I truly believe that crystals have been a poignant part of my spiritual growth, and I'm so passionate in bringing them out of the shadows and introducing people to their magnificent energies.

Give them a try yourself.

What have you got to lose?

Activity

Start by selecting a crystal that aligns with a current manifestation goal.

Create a small, dedicated space where you can sit quietly and undisturbed.

You might choose to light a candle or play soft music to define this space as sacred.

Hold your crystal in your hands, close your eyes and take a few deep breaths to centre yourself.

Clearly state your intention, either aloud or in your mind and visualise it coming to fruition.

Feel the emotions associated with achieving this goal, letting them fill you completely.

Imagine your crystal absorbing these intentions and emotions, becoming a beacon for your desires.

And then conclude your ritual by expressing gratitude to the Universe for its endless abundance and support.

Leave your crystal in the space you've created for as long as your intuition guides you to, allowing it to continue working on your behalf.

Chapter 8

Achieving Your Goals Using Vision Boards

Imagine you're about to set off and drive to a new destination on unfamiliar roads. Before you even leave your home, you're going to need a map with clear directions for how to get to where you want to go, as, without them, you're just aimless, hoping for the best.

In life, our goals are our destinations while a vision board is the map that keeps them in clear view and us in the right direction. Vision boards can clarify your deepest desires and maintain a focus on them, ensuring you navigate through life's twists and turns directly towards your goals.

Much like you must visualise the route to navigate, we use visualisation to carve out our path to success. Visualisation isn't merely daydreaming, but an active, purposeful exercise that engages the brain in a powerful way.

When we visualise achieving our goals, our brain works to align our actions with these visualisations.

Visualisation is the practice of imagining what you want to achieve in vivid detail, as if it were already true. It's a potent form of mental practice used by everyone from athletes to CEOs because it harnesses the power of our subconscious mind. Studies show that, just by visualising what to do, athletes enhance their actual performance.[13] Similarly, when we consistently see images representing our desires, our mind works tirelessly towards making these images a reality.

Most of you reading this will try to make excuses for not visualising. One of my friends, Nikki, is absolutely horrific with it. I keep telling her, "It'll take maybe two to three minutes per night in bed, just before you head off to sleep," and she tells me she just doesn't have the time.

The challenge with visualisation often stems from more than just our busy schedules, like my friend Nikki experiences. Many of us carry a bit of doubt deep inside about whether these techniques really work, or perhaps we just underestimate the power of our own thoughts. It's like having a little voice inside our heads telling us not to bother because it might not lead anywhere. This scepticism can act like a barrier, keeping us from fully embracing the practice of visualisation.

Ignoring the power of visualisation can leave our goals feeling a bit blurry, and our motivation might start to dip. Visualisation is like setting your GPS to success – it clarifies your destination and fires up your drive to get there.

By not regularly picturing our achievements, we miss the trick of syncing up our deepest desires with our daily actions and just might stick to what's familiar instead of reaching for what's possible. Visualisation isn't just daydreaming. It's a vital practice that prepares our mind to go after what we want, turning that "maybe one day" into "let's make this happen."

The second your head hits that pillow and you turn over to go to sleep, close your eyes and visualise. It's that simple! This is such a potent and powerful time for you to do this as you drift off to sleep, and you're using no extra time because you're already winding down for bed anyway.

Visualisation is such a powerful tool to help you get into the mindset of someone who's already achieved what they want in life. When we visualise our desired outcomes, we begin to see the possibility of achieving them. Our mind sets itself to work on making these visualised goals a reality, influencing our decision-making and bolstering our confidence and motivation.

In a world filled with distractions and constant challenges, setting clear and attainable goals can sometimes seem overwhelming. However, one of the most effective tools I've discovered in manifesting my desires and achieving my goals is using vision boards to help me get there. It's about setting intentions that resonate deeply with your personal aspirations and using them as a catalyst for action.

A vision board is more than just a collage of random images. It's a curated collection of pictures, words, and items that symbolise your dreams and goals.

Back in 2012, well before my spiritual journey started, I made my very first vision board with images of things for me to work toward as a reminder of why I was in my 9-5 on days I felt deflated. This was long before I had any knowledge of the Law of Attraction, and I did this solely for a boost of motivation in life. For it, I downloaded some images from Google and Pinterest, and I used a photo printing app to have them delivered to my house. I got scissor-happy and, using some glue, stuck them to a sheet of an A4 card. I placed a picture of a little Jack Russell on there, because at the time I had no doggy companion in my life, and I was desperate to have one. I also had some symbolic pictures on there of materialistic things such as cash, a nice beach symbolising a lovely holiday, the interior of a nice new car, as well as many pictures of my dream home.

I even put a screenshot of my bank statement on there, but using the magic of Photoshop, I erased my actual balance, and typed out the balance that I wanted to see. I found quotes on Google, such as affirmations that supported and encapsulated all of my goals, and I placed those in the centre of my vision board to use as my mantra.

The most important thing to remember with a vision board is that you might not necessarily know how you're going to bring your goals to fruition and bring these individual things into your life, and that's OK! You have to know that you want it and then things will fall into place – like I always say, forget the how; let the Universe sort that out. You wouldn't order from Amazon and then wonder how your item is going to get to you, spending all your time worrying about it actually arriving. You place your order and you know it'll come eventually.

I remember taking photocopies of my vision board on the copier at work (thank you, NHS!) and placing a copy next to my bed, a copy on my desk, a copy in my car, and a smaller version in my wallet. As the years passed by, I just forgot about it and got on with life.

Over the years, they ended up as most bits of paper do, being used to scribble down other notes or eventually being thrown out when decluttering.

During the pandemic in 2020, I came across one of these printouts in my drawers as I was cleaning out my desk to start working from home. When I looked at my vision board, I was actually shocked.

The car interior was the car I was driving at the time, and yet there I was, looking for a newer car by that point! I hadn't even realised that my dream car from years ago was now mine, because I was too wrapped up in wanting the next best thing. The photo of the Jack Russell was eerily similar to JJ, the dog I now had, with almost identical markings. The bank balance on my printout was now my annual salary, having moved jobs internally a few times since then. I'd been on the holiday of a lifetime, travelling around Thailand, which was where the photo was taken of the beach on my vision board, and, to top it all off, the photos of the interior of the home on my board were bizarrely alike to the house that I was now living in.

It was so weird.

All these changes between 2012 and 2020 happened so gradually that I didn't even realise that I was living the dream that 2012 me had always been striving towards.

I felt stupid. It struck me then how easy it is to overlook our achievements and blessings, really making me reflect on the fact that no matter what we're given in life, we're always chasing something better, when really, we should be sitting back and smelling the roses. I had spent years chasing after dreams and scarcely noticed when they transitioned into realities. This revelation was both humbling and enlightening. It brought to light a deeper truth about human nature: Our endless pursuit of "more" often blinds us to the wonders we currently possess.

This epiphany led me to a shift in mindset: It's equally important to pause, reflect, and appreciate the journey. As we move forward in life, it's crucial not only to continue setting goals but also to dream big and appreciate what we have in the here and now. The milestones we reach should be celebrated and savoured, not merely checked off a list and forgotten in the rush towards the next big thing.

Since 2020, my vision boards and goal-setting techniques have led to remarkable achievements in both my personal and professional life. From career advancements that seemed only a dream to enriching personal relationships and achieving long-held fitness goals, these visual and written declarations have been instrumental. I also now acknowledge and celebrate my progress, no matter how small, as I've learned that celebrating milestones can boost motivation and reinforce those positive behaviours within myself.

I like to ensure that I have a mixture on my vision boards of materialistic goals and also emotionally fulfilling ones such as a photo representing a happy, healthy family or positive mental health.

I now ensure that I tell people what my goals are, and I show them my vision board, so that people know what I'm working towards. There are so many benefits of sharing intentions with a friend, family member, or a community group. Shout your goals from the rooftops because sharing both creates a sense of accountability and provides the support from others that we sometimes need.

I then came across the idea of using vision boards for manifestation back in 2016 when I read *The Secret*, in which there are various examples of people who have made vision boards and then forgotten about them – then years later they find them and realise that everything on their vision board has manifested into something real.

We all know by now that the Law of Attraction is a lot about your subconscious mind. The way I like to think about this is by imagining an iceberg. Your conscious mind is the tip while your subconscious is the rest of the iceberg under the water. It's so important to remember the huge chunk of your brain that you aren't consciously using. By having this vision board and constantly looking at the images, the symbols, the words, the cohesive message is ingrained into your subconscious to the point that every single day without realising it you'll be doing things to get closer to these goals, whether you realise it or not.

The best way to start your own is by writing down all of your goals for a set amount of time – so for example, think about the next two to five years of your life and then create a huge brainstorm or mind map in which you can list all your goals. You could even have headings for each area of life such as

career, money, health goals, material goals, relationship goals...
anything that you want to achieve.

To do this, I find it best to meditate to explore your future and to
look at your values and your lifelong commitments. I find that
asking myself thought-provoking questions really helps me to
get to the nitty-gritty of what I truly want.

What kind of person do you want to be?

What values do you want your life to affirm?

When you look back on the other side of your life, what do you
want to see?

What is most important to you in life?

What kind of person are you becoming?

Activity

Grab yourself a blank sheet of paper and a pen. Gently close your eyes for a moment and clear all thoughts from your head.

Imagine yourself travelling forward in time until you arrive exactly one year from today.

What do you see around you?

What can you hear and feel?

Where are you?

Who are you?

What would you say to your future self?

Where are you in terms of your dreams, your connection to your hopes and prayers?

Where are you with your physical health and how do you feel about it?

How is your relationship with your family?

What is your relationship with your friends like?

What new people are in your life now that just a year ago you dreamed of having in your life?

Where are you with your belief in your own worth and power?

How courageous are you?

What are you committed to?

How big do you smile?

Do you feel lighter or heavier?

More alive or less alive?

Imagine if this was all true – if everything that you just answered in your head and felt in your heart were guaranteed to come true – how would you be sitting right now? Where would your shoulders be? What kind of facial expression would you have? How would you be breathing?

Now, gently open your eyes and take a look at the blank sheet of paper in front of you, making a list of how you're living this time next year. You can write this all down in linear or bullet points, as a mind map, poetry, a brainstorm, or whatever works for you.

Setting clear intentions acts as a roadmap guiding our actions and decisions throughout the year. Intentions can provide focus and clarity, which will reduce the feeling of being overwhelmed by having too many goals.

I'd like to stress the importance here of aligning your intentions with your personal core values; when intentions are in harmony with our values, they feel more authentic and achievable. To do this, I'd definitely suggest using visualisation to imagine how fulfilling these intentions will feel to you.

Be specific, but remain flexible.

This really confuses some people when I say this. What I mean is, try to be specific enough so that your intentions have direction, but also flexible enough to adapt to changing circumstances, because nothing will ever 100% go the way that you planned.

For example, rather than just intending to be healthy, you might aim to incorporate more fruits and vegetables into meals, or engage in physical activity three times a week.

Once you've decided what you want – what you really, really want – write it down. Write down your intentions. This act can make intentions feel more concrete and memorable. You can incorporate these worded intentions onto your vision board where you can see them daily. Writing them down also allows you to reflect back on them at a later date and see how far you've actually come.

Once I completed this particular activity and gathered my pictures, symbolising what I wanted, I would look at these images and feel super inspired – it always makes me want to work so much harder to achieve my goals and see what can be achieved when I put my mind to something.

How to Create an Effective Vision Board

In a world rife with distractions and challenges, setting clear and attainable goals can sometimes feel overwhelming. However, one of the most effective tools I've found for manifesting desires and achieving goals is a vision board.

A vision board is more than a collection of images. It's a curated assemblage of pictures, words, and symbols that represent your dreams and aspirations.

It acts as a catalyst for action, setting intentions that resonate deeply with your personal goals.

Set clear intentions. Before you start searching for images or items, take a moment to clearly define what you want to achieve. Write down specific goals in areas such as career, relationships, health, finances, or personal growth.

Gather your materials. You'll need a board (cork, poster, or digital), scissors, glue, magazines, printouts, and any other items that inspire you.

Find images that resonate. Look for images that closely represent your aspirations. These images should evoke a strong emotional response, as emotion is a powerful motivator in achieving goals.

Arrange and affix. Lay out your images and items on the board. Move them around until you feel that their arrangement visually represents your goals. Then, fix them on the board.

Place your vision board. Put your vision board in a place where you will see it every day. This visibility reminds you of your goals and reinforces your commitment to achieving them.

Complement your vision board by writing down your goals. This practice is just as powerful as visualisation itself. The act of writing makes your goals concrete and signals to your brain that they're important to you. Keep a goal journal, or make a habit of daily goal affirmations.

To make my vision boards as of late, I've started to use a private Instagram account. I choose whatever photos I want to put onto my board, upload them all into the app on my private profile, and then I can write underneath each one in the caption why I'd love to have that goal come to fruition. Once that goal has been achieved, I update the caption to reflect this.

It's a super easy, efficient, and free way to get started with creating your own vision board. I often screenshot my Instagram profile grid and set this as my phone wallpaper too so that I see my goals each time I pick up my phone. I even have a digital version on my laptop desktop screen. If you prefer to, you could always get yourself a nice corkboard, like in the '90s, and get some photos printed, pinning each one to it, so you have something physical. The aim is to place your vision board where you're going to see it daily, and whether you notice it consciously or subconsciously, it's there!

Regular Check-ins

For accountability purposes, setting yourself regular check-in intervals to reflect on your intentions, such as the start of each month, will really help keep you on track. This is your time to adjust your intentions as needed, making any necessary tweaks, and this is your opportunity to remember that it's okay to evolve and change to fit in with life.

After adapting my process, the vision board that I created in 2022 was crazy in so many ways. I really stepped out of my comfort zone and attempted to bring my vision board to life by placing images on my vision board that included myself in them. In doing this, I went out and test-drove a car that I had no intention of purchasing due to its incredibly high price. Whilst I was out in the car, I pulled over and took photos of my own tattooed arm on the steering wheel, my legs on the foot pedals, and a selfie of myself pretending to drive. Once I returned to the showroom, I got the salesman to take photos of me beside the car, and much to his delight, too, as I stood in different poses thinking I was on the red carpet getting photographed by paparazzi!

As I placed these images on my vision board, I knew that instead of it now just being a photo of a car, they were my arms on that steering wheel, they were my legs on those pedals. That was me physically driving that car! Doing this really helped to bring my vision board to life. They were no longer just images, just as vision boards and goal-setting aren't simply about hoping for a better future. They're about creating that future, making it reality. Through the simple yet profound acts of selecting images, arranging thoughts, and affirming desires, we set the stage for manifesting our dreams. As we shout our goals from the rooftops, or more precisely, from our walls and journals, we invite the energy of achievement and success into our lives.

Within six months of placing those images on my vision board, I'd taken action and gone through the paperwork of how much the car would actually cost me. Yes, the monthly payments were more than my current car, but that car was on its last legs and was costing us so much in unexpected repairs and bills.

I sat down one night and went through my finances to see where I could make cuts here and there, and by doing this, I realised that I could actually afford it comfortably. I placed a deposit and, just three months later, once it had been delivered to the showroom, I went and picked up my very own Range Rover Velar.

That was such a pivotal moment for me.

Not only was it the very first time I'd bought a brand new car, but it was also the very first time I'd ever spent that kind of money on something for myself. It felt like all the time and hard work I put into my business, whilst still working full-time for the NHS, was finally paying off.

Did it bring me the pleasure that I thought it would?

Did I elevate into a state of sheer enlightenment?

No.

In fact, it made me realise that my vision board should be filled with things that make my heart sing, rather than materialistic goals of me attempting to keep up with the Joneses. It enabled me to reflect on what I truly wanted in both my business and personal life and ensure that the next vision board I created was filled with more emotionally fulfilling things, so that I was striving for happiness, rather than seeking outside validation, all for the sake of a photo for likes on social media.

While walking my dog one day in 2023 through a beautiful, private estate just west of Newcastle, I was struck by the tranquil and calming energy of the little village, captivated by its stunning scenery and surroundings. As I walked by one of the houses, I said to Jonny, "That's my dream home. How gorgeous is it?" and proceeded to take photos of myself in front of it, smiling away, probably whilst the owners were scowling out of their windows at me doing so. I popped these photos on my vision board a week or so later, and after doing a little research by looking at houses in that area, I just knew there was no way we could afford a mortgage on one of them – the prices were five times what we are currently paying!

I felt a sense of defeat wash over me because it made me realise that it was a goal out of my current reach.

"One day!" I said to myself.

I remember setting myself a Rightmove alert for all houses in that postcode area, just in case.

The vision board, including the images of this house, was on my phone screen, my laptop screen, beside my desk at work – I was seeing images of this house daily.

About three months after doing this, I was lying in bed late on a Friday evening and an email popped up stating there was a new home up for sale in that area. I clicked on the link, and to my surprise, it was the house from my vision board: my dream home!

I couldn't believe it.

It wasn't a house that looked like my dream home.

It wasn't a house that was similar to my dream home.

It was the same exact house!

And what's more is that the listing had included photos of the inside of the property, so I could now add these to my vision board too! It was stunning – and I could now start to visualise what it would be like to physically live there, walking around each of the rooms in my mind's eye.

Naturally, I rang up to book a viewing at the earliest opportunity, but with the property value being way out of our current budget, Jonny said that he couldn't come with me and lied about pretending to have those kinds of funds!

I could have said to myself, "Yeah, he's right," and given up at the first hurdle, but I thought, "No. This house is actually incredible, and I want to live there!" So I went on my own to the viewing, and to my surprise, the lady showing me around the house was the current owner. As she led me around her home, I took photos in every room, trying to incorporate myself into them as though the house was mine. I had to explain to her what I was doing at one point, as I'm sure she probably thought, "This guy is going to burgle my house tonight!"

I took out pots and pans in her kitchen and had her take photos of me pretending to cook, I sat at the table and chairs in her garden and had her take photos of me with my laptop pretending to work...I even took photos of myself sitting on the toilet in her bathroom, and pretending to wash myself in her shower. I'm pretty sure she was about to dial 999 at one point. Again, just like with the car, I did all of this to bring my vision board to life.

At the time of writing this book, we've not yet moved into this property. However, the price is reducing week on week and to this day, they've still not found a buyer! I truly believe that it's on the cards and that the Universe will move Heaven and Earth to ensure this happens one day for us.

Reflecting on My Vision Board Success

I had a few tears reflecting on just how far I'd come using my vision board process. I remember at the start of 2023, I'd just been booked for my first-ever keynote speaker slot.

On the day that I was pulling the presentation together, I was listening to Katy Perry's "Déjà Vu" – there's a line in the chorus where Katy sings, "Every day's the same, the definition of insane, I think I'm running on a loop, déjà vu". Hearing this made me think, "I don't want the next 12 months to be another carbon copy of the year I've just had, I actually want to grow as a person, as a business, I want to develop myself and I want to land in 12 months time, in a whole new space in life".

Tony Robbins once said, "The scariest place to be this time next year is in the same place as you are right now." Hearing that quote lit such a rocket under my backside that I thought to myself, "I'm going to fully commit to this vision board process for the next 12 months."

Here's what I achieved in those 12 months from taking inspired action to achieve the goals on my vision board:

I started the year by retiring my mam, Angela, who now works for me one day a week.

I employed an admin assistant who now packs all of my orders.

I hired an admin assistant who deals with all my emails and general life admin.

I now own the car of my dreams.

I started the adoption process with my partner, Jonny.

I was featured in three issues of *British Vogue* in their health and well-being campaign.

I was asked to speak at Stella McCartney's pride event.

I was then asked to also speak at her January retreat for new staff in Milan.

I held an event in London at the Barbican Centre for 800 people with Fran, which we sold out.

I had a £27,000 order for crystal table centrepieces from Chanel for their Summer Ball.

And I even got the ball rolling with a book deal for this new book....

These are just some of the things that I accomplished in those 12 months because those are just all the big things. There are all the smaller things too that I've not mentioned there, such as consistently showing up in my business and growing my social media accounts daily, and so on.

When I list all my large accomplishments like that it astounds me that had I not followed this vision board process, I might have found myself in the exact same place as I was 12 months prior, without that growth, expansion, and transformation.

Time-Specific Vision Boards

If there's a specific goal that you want to achieve, sometimes even making specific vision boards for the month or so ahead can be particularly useful.

For example, in January, seeing all of my goals visually for that month actually in front of my eyes gives me something that I can work towards, rather than filling my head with the dread we all usually feel at the start of the new year. If you had a specific long-term goal you could create a vision board based around that goal itself.

For example, now that I want to buy that nice house in the next couple of years, I've created a board entirely dedicated to that – where I've placed more images of my dream home, complete with furniture, garden items, furnishings – which is a lot more specific and in alignment with my goal. Once I've created my vision boards and put them everywhere I'll see them, I don't just assume that's enough.

When I come to meditate or do any kind of visualisation, I'll look at the vision board that I've created and bring it to life through emotions such as joy, happiness, excitement and a sense of wonder. That picture of the beach symbolising the holiday? You better believe I'm visualising and imagining how the sun feels on my skin, what I can hear, what it feels like to be carefree and on holiday. Bring your vision board to life!

Use your senses to help you do this. Give it some real emotion and feeling, give your love to it, and whatever is on your board will come to fruition. This is actually a really fun process. It just depends on your personal preference which type of vision board you choose to create, whether it be one board encapsulating all of your goals and desires or targeting specific ones. The choice is yours!

I save each board that I create into a folder on my phone, and every time I'm lacking motivation, or maybe just feel like I need some clarity, I'll go into the folder and have a look through my boards and feel that inspiration deep down inside. This helps to put a smile on my face and helps me gain focus on why I'm doing what I do.

It's not just about doing a vision board, and that's it – done and dusted, never to be looked at ever again. It's all about formulating and taking those next actionable steps. Start with small, achievable goals to build your confidence. Remember that obstacles like doubt, procrastination, and fear of failure will always creep up on you. But also remember the importance of having consistency and patience in the process.

It won't happen overnight, but if you don't take action now, it won't happen at all.

Activity

Create a vision board using one of the methods I suggested.

Decide on your timescale, whether it be for the next three, six months, a year, two years or five years ahead.

Ask yourself, "What do I truly want in life?" and write it all down.

Bring your board to life with images, text, and symbols that represent your desires.

Put it somewhere you'll see it each and every day, and take those steps towards achieving your goals.

Share your vision board with me if you're feeling brave, tagging @cannycrystals across social media.

Chapter 9

Understanding the Energy of Subliminal Affirmations

Imagine you're dressed up and ready for a night out at the city's most exclusive club.

As you approach the entrance, your excitement builds. You can hear the thumping bass, see the vibrant lights flashing inside and feel the contagious energy of the people in line with you. But just as you think you're about to step into this world of fun, you face a roadblock: the bouncer.

His job is to scrutinise everyone, deciding who gets in and who doesn't.

Tonight, he looks at you and says, without hesitation, "You're not getting in." Just like that, your night takes a sharp turn. You're left outside, denied entry to the experience you were so eagerly anticipating.

But you're not one to give up that easily.

Instead of walking away, you decide to explore the perimeter of the club. You stumble upon a back door, slightly ajar and unguarded. A surge of hope flows through you. Quietly, you slip in, bypassing the bouncer completely. Suddenly, you're inside the club, free to enjoy the music, dance, and atmosphere just as you had hoped.

This scenario is more than just a story. It's a metaphor for how subliminal affirmations work with our minds.

The bouncer represents your conscious mind, which is often very selective and protective, guarding what it lets in. If a new idea doesn't fit with your existing beliefs or identity, it gets blocked. But the back door represents your subconscious mind – a more accessible route where new ideas can enter without facing the same scrutiny or rejection.

The Conscious Mind vs. The Subconscious Mind

To truly understand the power of subliminal affirmations, we need to differentiate between the conscious and subconscious parts of our minds.

Think of the conscious mind as the "gatekeeper." It filters information based on our existing beliefs, experiences, and perceptions. It's like a critical editor, always on the lookout for errors, contradictions, and inconsistencies. If a thought or idea doesn't align with what you already believe, your conscious mind tends to reject or dismiss it.

This is why, even when we try to use positive affirmations consciously, we might feel a pushback – a voice inside that says, "That's not true!" or "That doesn't apply to me!"

Your subconscious mind, on the other hand, is different. It operates much like a sponge, absorbing everything it comes into contact with without judgement. It stores your deepest beliefs, memories, habits and experiences. It influences how you perceive the world, how you react to it, and ultimately the decisions you make.

Because it doesn't filter information the same way the conscious mind does, it's more open to influence – especially when the information is repeated often. This is where subliminal affirmations come in.

How Subliminal Affirmations Work

Subliminal affirmations are positive messages embedded in audio or visual content at a low volume or quick speed, designed to bypass the conscious mind's critical filter.

Just like the metaphor, subliminal affirmations work by sneaking past the "bouncer" of your conscious mind and reaching the subconscious. Imagine listening to an audio track that contains soothing sounds like ocean waves or relaxing music. Embedded within that track, at a level below what you can consciously hear, are positive affirmations such as "I am confident", "I attract success", or "I am calm and relaxed."

Because these affirmations bypass the conscious mind, they go straight to the subconscious, where they can slowly start to shape your beliefs and behaviours.

Put simply, subliminal affirmations work by tapping into the subconscious mind's natural ability to absorb and integrate information. Over time, as these messages are repeated, they start to overwrite negative or limiting beliefs and replace them with more empowering ones.

The Science Behind Subliminal Affirmations

Subliminal affirmations are based on the principles of neuroplasticity, the brain's ability to reorganise itself by forming new neural connections throughout life. Neuroplasticity indicates that our brains are not static: They're incredibly adaptable and can change in response to new information, experiences, and repeated stimuli.

When we listen to subliminal affirmations, we're exposing our minds to positive messages repeatedly. This repetition allows these messages to penetrate the depths of our subconscious mind, where they begin to form new neural pathways.

If we were to look in the mirror for example and just say an affirmation aloud like, "I'm a money magnet, money flows to me effortlessly and I'm a wealthy person," our conscious mind might respond internally with, "What are you talking about Mart? No you're not!", and immediately dismiss our affirmations, closing our mind from developing itself. Whereas when these same messages are delivered to our brains subconsciously, we haven't got those "bouncers" or "security guards" saying, "No, sorry – you're not getting in!"

Over time, this process can help rewire the brain, reinforcing new thought patterns and beliefs. The more we listen, the more these new patterns have a chance to take hold, leading to a transformation in how we think, feel and behave.

This concept is closely related to "repetition compulsion," a psychological phenomenon where repeated exposure to a stimulus makes it more familiar, accepted, and ultimately, a part of our belief system.

By repeatedly exposing the subconscious mind to positive affirmations, we're more likely to adopt these new beliefs as truths. For instance, listening to a subliminal track with affirmations like "I am worthy of success" or "I embrace opportunities for growth" over an extended period can help shift a person's mindset from one of scarcity to one of abundance.

What Subliminal Affirmations Can and Cannot Do

Many people have misconceptions about subliminal affirmations, often believing they're a form of mind control, magical tools that can instantly change someone's life, or inherently manipulative tactics used to force unwanted behaviours or thoughts.

Let's break down these myths and provide a clear understanding of what subliminal affirmations are and what they are not.

Myth 1: Subliminal affirmations are magical or mind-control tools.

One of the most persistent myths is that subliminal affirmations have the power to control our minds or change our behaviour without our consent. This idea often comes from sensationalised portrayals in movies or conspiracy theories about subliminal messages in advertising and propaganda. The reality, however, is far more grounded.

What subliminals actually do: Subliminal affirmations work by subtly influencing the subconscious mind through repeated, positive messaging. The subconscious mind is highly receptive to repeated input, but it doesn't automatically accept or act on information unless it aligns with the individual's existing beliefs and intentions. Subliminals do not have the power to force someone to do something against their will or values. Research shows that subliminal messages can have a mild, subconscious influence, but they do not override a person's conscious decisions or deeply held beliefs. For instance, while a subliminal message might nudge someone toward feeling more confident or relaxed, it can't make someone suddenly quit their job or fall in love without any conscious consideration. The mind is far more complex and resilient than that.

Myth 2: Subliminals are a quick fix to all problems.

Another common misconception is that subliminal affirmations provide an instant solution to problems or that they work like a magic spell to bring about desired changes with little to no effort. This myth can be particularly misleading and can lead to disappointment if people expect quick results without understanding the need for consistency and openness.

Reality check: Consistency and effort matter. Just like any tool for personal growth – be it meditation, therapy, or exercise – subliminal affirmations require time, consistency, and commitment to show tangible results. They're not a one-time solution or an effortless path to success. Instead, subliminals are more like planting seeds in the garden of your mind. They need time to take root, grow, and flourish. The effectiveness of subliminals can vary widely from person to person. Some may notice subtle shifts in their thoughts and behaviours after a few weeks, while others might need months of regular listening to see more significant changes. The key is to understand that subliminals work subtly and gradually by influencing subconscious patterns, not by delivering immediate or dramatic results.

Myth 3: Subliminal affirmations are inherently manipulative.

There's also a belief that subliminal affirmations are inherently manipulative or that they can be used unethically to manipulate others without their awareness. While it is true that subliminal messages have been used unethically in some historical contexts, such as in certain advertising campaigns or propaganda, this is not representative of their use in personal development.

Ethical use of subliminals: When used ethically, subliminal affirmations are tools for self-improvement, designed to help us overcome limiting beliefs, build confidence, or achieve personal goals. Ethical use involves transparency, informed consent, and a focus on positive, empowering messages. Subliminals should never be used to manipulate others' thoughts or behaviours without their knowledge and consent. When someone consciously chooses to use subliminal affirmations as part of their self-development practice, they're actively participating in the process of change. They're not being manipulated, but are instead empowering themselves by aligning their conscious desires with subconscious programming. The intention behind the use is key to distinguishing ethical from unethical use.

Real-life Examples of Subliminal Affirmations

The effectiveness of subliminal affirmations isn't just a theoretical concept. Many people, including myself, have experienced significant positive changes by incorporating these powerful tools into their lives. Let me share a personal story to illustrate this.

At one point in 2022, I found myself vaping again out of sheer boredom. I had quit smoking in 2012 and hadn't touched any form of nicotine for nearly a decade. But suddenly, the old habit began to creep back in. I felt the addiction slowly taking hold, and within a few weeks, I was vaping more frequently. I knew I had to do something to break this cycle. I decided to create a subliminal audio focused on overcoming addiction. I embedded affirmations like "I am free from addiction," "I control my urges" and "My body is healthy and pure."

I listened to this track daily, especially during moments of temptation or stress. Within a short period, I noticed a dramatic shift. The urge to vape diminished, and my resolve to stay nicotine-free strengthened. I didn't touch any more nicotine after starting to listen to this subliminal!

While I'm not saying subliminals are a magic cure, they certainly provide a powerful way to reprogram the mind and give yourself the best possible chance of a positive outcome.

The Power of Repetition and Consistency

One of the most critical factors in the effectiveness of subliminal affirmations is repetition. Just as negative beliefs can form through repeated negative self-talk or experiences, positive beliefs can be instilled through repeated exposure to positive messages.

It's important to understand that these changes don't happen overnight. The process is gradual, often requiring weeks or even months of consistent listening to see significant results. However, just as small drops of water can eventually fill a bucket, regular exposure to subliminal affirmations can lead to profound changes in how we perceive ourselves and the world around us.

Imagine the possibilities if, by simply listening to a set of subliminal affirmations, you could start to change your mindset, behaviours, and life outcomes.

Subliminal affirmations can be incredibly versatile and effective for various personal development goals, including:

Increasing wealth. By listening to affirmations focused on financial abundance, you might find yourself more attuned to opportunities for making money, saving, or investing wisely. Over time, you could develop a wealth-oriented mindset that helps you attract more financial opportunities.

Improving health. Subliminals can support a healthy lifestyle by reinforcing beliefs around healthy eating, regular exercise, and overall wellness. Repeated affirmations like "I enjoy nourishing my body with healthy food" or "I am committed to regular exercise" can help establish new, healthier habits.

Reducing anxiety. Subliminal affirmations can also help calm an anxious mind by reinforcing beliefs around calmness, safety, and resilience. Affirmations like, "I am safe and secure" or "I can handle whatever comes my way" can help reduce anxiety and promote a sense of inner peace.

Enhancing relationships. Relationships can also benefit from subliminal affirmations that promote love, empathy and effective communication. For instance, affirmations like "I am loving and compassionate" or "I communicate clearly and honestly" can help improve interpersonal dynamics.

Creating Your Own Subliminal Affirmation Tracks

One of the best ways to make subliminal affirmations work for you is creating your own personalised tracks.

While there are many pre-recorded subliminal audios available online, creating your own allows you to tailor the affirmations to your specific goals and needs. Here's a simple step-by-step guide on how to create your own subliminal affirmation track:

Identify your goals. Determine the area of your life you want to improve – whether it's confidence, health, wealth, relationships or another aspect. Be specific about what you want to achieve.

Write positive affirmations. Craft affirmations that are positive, present-tense and specific. For example, instead of saying, "I will be confident", use "I am confident and self-assured." Keep them short and direct.

Record your affirmations. Use a voice recorder app on your phone or computer to record your affirmations. Speak clearly and slowly. You can use a soft, soothing tone to make the affirmations more relaxing.

Layer affirmations with background music. Choose calming background sounds like ocean waves, rain or ambient music. Use audio editing software to layer your recorded affirmations beneath the background music at a low volume, so they're just below the level of conscious hearing.

Listen consistently. Make it a habit to listen to your subliminal track daily, during your commute, while working or as you fall asleep. Consistency is key to seeing results.

Combining Subliminal Affirmations with Other Techniques

Subliminal affirmations can be incredibly powerful on their own, but when combined with other self-improvement techniques, their effectiveness can be significantly amplified.

Visualisation. Combining subliminal affirmations with visualisation techniques allows the subconscious to hear and visually simulate the positive changes, making the affirmations more tangible and believable. For instance, while listening to affirmations about success, visualise yourself achieving your goals, receiving accolades or feeling confident. This combination can help reinforce the desired outcome more powerfully.

Meditation. Incorporating subliminal affirmations into meditation sessions can deepen relaxation and enhance focus, providing a fertile ground for the affirmations to take root. During meditation, the mind is more relaxed and open, which can make subliminal messages even more effective. Try listening to subliminals that focus on inner peace and mindfulness while meditating to double the impact.

Traditional affirmations. Using subliminal affirmations alongside traditional affirmations – spoken or written – ensures consistent messaging to both the conscious and subconscious mind, reinforcing those desired changes from multiple angles.

This can be particularly effective when trying to instil a new belief or habit.

Practical Tips for Using Subliminal Affirmations

Many people wonder how to fit subliminal affirmations into their already busy lives. The good news is that it doesn't require any extra time! You can listen to subliminal affirmations during your commute, while doing chores, exercising or even as you drift off to sleep.

That is to say, consider your daily life and identify pockets of time where you can listen to subliminal affirmations. It could be while you're getting ready in the morning, on your lunch break, or as you wind down before bed. Consistency is key, so try to make it a non-negotiable part of your routine.

One highly effective strategy is to play subliminal affirmations while you sleep. Your subconscious mind is still active and receptive, and this can be an effortless way to integrate affirmations into your routine. If you live alone, play the subliminals out loud on your phone. If you share a space, consider using headphones or a sleep mask with built-in speakers. Imagine getting six to eight hours of subconscious programming every night!

If you find it difficult to listen for long periods, break your listening sessions into shorter intervals. For example, you can listen to subliminal affirmations for ten minutes in the morning, another ten minutes during lunch, and another ten minutes in the evening. Short and frequent sessions can still have a positive impact over time because the cumulative effect builds up.

If you exercise regularly, use that time to listen to subliminal affirmations. Whether you're running, lifting weights or doing yoga, playing affirmations in the background can enhance your mindset and focus. You can even use subliminals while doing mundane tasks like cleaning, cooking, or gardening.

The beauty of subliminal affirmations is that you can listen to more than one type at once. For example, you might choose to listen to affirmations for self-love in the morning, wealth and abundance during the day and gratitude in the evening. There are no strict rules. It's all about what resonates with you and aligns with your goals.

Real-life Testimonials

I remember when I first heard about the use of subliminal affirmations whilst undergoing a module in Denise Duffield-Thomas' Money Bootcamp course. I was intrigued and simply thought, "How can listening to this peaceful track filled with ocean noises and bird sounds enhance my wealth and abundance?" I was sceptical to say the very least, but I continued to listen as instructed: every day for around 21 days.

The mindset shifts that I experienced within those three weeks were phenomenal. I started to find random banknotes in my clothes pockets that I couldn't even remember putting there in the first place. I had a refund on an item I'd bought a few weeks prior as it had been reduced further in a sale. I received money in abundance through my business. I almost felt like a money magnet. Wealth and abundance were flowing to me like never before!

Did I tell all of my friends and family about it? Straight away in fact!

Did any of them listen to me and start listening to their own subliminal affirmation tracks? Did they, heck!

I pondered for a while about how to introduce subliminal affirmations to people without it sounding like some wishy-washy method, and I realised that I needed to find a way to make it as relatable and as practical as possible. After all, the proof was in my own experience, but not everyone is ready to dive into something that sounds more like magic than methodology.

Many individuals have reported huge changes in their lives due to the use of subliminal affirmations. For example, one of my clients, a high school student, was struggling with concentration and motivation. She began listening to subliminal affirmations specifically focused on enhancing concentration and academic success. After a few weeks, not only did her grades improve, but she also reported feeling more focused, less stressed and more confident in her abilities.

Another example involves a professional athlete I worked with who was dealing with performance anxiety. We crafted a set of subliminal affirmations focused on confidence, resilience and peak performance. Within months, she saw significant improvements in her performance, won multiple competitions and even surpassed her own expectations in terms of personal records.

These experiences taught me an invaluable lesson about human psychology: People may resist what they don't understand, but once they see tangible benefits, their walls come down. It reinforced my belief in the power of sharing knowledge and experience transparently, helping illuminate the path for others to follow and explore the transformative potential of their own minds.

Creating a Receptive Mindset

For subliminal affirmations to work effectively, you need to cultivate a receptive mindset. This involves being open to the possibility of change, patient with the process, and committed to personal growth.

Being open to change means letting go of rigid beliefs or expectations about how change should look. It involves trusting the process and allowing the subconscious mind to absorb the affirmations without overanalysing or doubting them. Openness can be fostered through practices like mindfulness, meditation, or simply being curious about the journey of self-discovery.

Patience is essential when working with subliminals. Unlike some instant gratification techniques, subliminals work subtly and gradually. Expecting immediate results can lead to frustration and abandonment of the practice. Recognising that meaningful change takes time can help users stay committed and observant of even the smallest shifts in their thoughts, feelings, or behaviours.

Just as with learning a new skill or building a habit, consistency is key to making subliminal affirmations effective. A few days of listening may not lead to noticeable changes, but weeks or months of consistent practice can create huge shifts in your life. Making a daily habit of listening to subliminals and combining them with other positive practices can strengthen their impact.

By understanding the myths and misconceptions, and recognising the importance of intent and belief, you can harness the full potential of subliminal affirmations to create meaningful, lasting change in your life.

Embrace the Power

By integrating subliminal affirmations into your daily routine, you can subtly but powerfully influence your subconscious mind to align with your goals. With time and consistency, these affirmations can help you build a more positive, confident and resilient mindset.

Subliminal affirmations are a gentle yet powerful way to tap into the potential of your mind and create meaningful change. So why not give them a try? Listen to them whenever you can, and watch as your life transforms in ways you never thought possible.

Activity

To truly harness the power of your subconscious mind and facilitate meaningful change in your life, I've developed an exclusive, free one-hour subliminal audio track, available at cannycrystalsacademy.co.uk/limitless.

This carefully crafted subliminal recording contains layered affirmations that are designed to penetrate your subconscious mind, promoting positive shifts in your attitudes and behaviours without your conscious awareness.

The subliminal is engineered to be played in the background while you engage in your everyday activities. Whether you're walking, performing housework or even working out at the gym, just play the track. The affirmations are set beneath layers of soothing audio, so they don't distract you from your tasks yet effectively reach the deeper levels of your mind.

For optimal results, commit to listening to this subliminal track for at least 21 consecutive days. This period helps cement the positive affirmations into your subconscious, facilitating a transformation that can manifest in various aspects of your life from increased positivity and motivation to improved wellbeing and personal achievements.

Witness the transformation as your subconscious begins to align more closely with your conscious goals, making the changes you desire not just possible, but inevitable.

Chapter 10
Tapping Into a Better Life

In the realm of manifestation, our emotional state acts as a powerful signal to the Universe. Positive emotions such as joy, love and excitement are believed to align us with the frequencies of abundance and success. Conversely, persistent negative emotions like fear, anxiety and doubt can attract more of the same, creating a cycle that can be hard to break.

Maintaining an emotional balance isn't just beneficial for mental and physical health. It's essential for effective manifestation.

What if I told you that by clearing blockages and reducing emotional distress, Emotional Freedom Techniques (EFT) help maintain a positive outlook and a higher vibration, conducive to attracting good things?

What if I said that with reduced emotional turmoil, your mental clarity and concentration improve, allowing you to maintain focus on your manifestation goals?

What if you found that by practising EFT, you felt less stress and emotional baggage, which led to better physical health, making you more energetic and active in pursuing your desires?

As you overcome emotional barriers and experience personal growth, your confidence in handling various life situations increases, and this is the beauty of this easy technique!

The principle behind EFT is based on the meridian points used in traditional acupuncture to treat physical and emotional ailments for over 5,000 years, but without the invasiveness of needles. Instead, tapping with the fingertips on these meridian endpoints inputs kinetic energy onto specific points while you think about your specific problem and vocalise positive affirmations.

Here's a simple breakdown of how EFT tapping can be performed:

Identify the issue. Before beginning, you must identify the issue you want to focus on. It's crucial to think about only one problem at a time to target your session effectively.

Test your initial intensity. Determine the initial intensity of your issue on a scale of 0 to 10, with 10 being the worst or most difficult.

Perform the setup. Perform the setup by crafting a statement that acknowledges the issue and expresses self-acceptance despite this problem. While continuously tapping the karate chop point on one hand, repeat your setup phrase three times aloud. An example setup phrase is: "Even though I feel this anxiety, I deeply and completely love and accept myself."

Try the sequence. Tap around five to seven times each on the designated meridian points while repeating a reminder phrase concerning your issue. Move through each point, starting from the top of the head, down to the eyebrow, side of the eye, under the eye, under the nose, the chin, the beginning of the collarbone, and under the arm.

Test your intensity again. At the end of a complete sequence, rate the intensity level of your issue again on a scale of 0 to 10. Compare it with the initial intensity level to see if it has changed and repeat until the intensity is significantly reduced or gone.

Imagine stepping into an amusement park and having your heart set on the most thrilling and hair-raising rollercoaster – the one that promises a mixture of anticipation and excitement! You've heard stories from friends about how good it is, how fast it goes and the weightlessness of its drops. As you secure yourself in the seat, a flutter of anxiety tingles through your entire body. The coaster lurches forward, and each twist and turn transforms your nervousness into adrenaline-fueled joy.

By the time the ride ends, you're laughing. Your initial apprehensions are now a distant memory, replaced by exhilaration and a newfound sense of victory. You did it: You rode that huge rollercoaster and turned your anxious thoughts into positive excitement.

This experience mirrors my initial encounter with EFT, or tapping, as it's often called. At a self-improvement workshop, feeling more like a sceptical observer at a magic show, I was unsure yet intrigued. The instructor, with her infectious energy, promised us a tool that could effortlessly transform our inner chaos into peace.

Deciding to embrace the unknown, I took the plunge into the world of EFT, not realising how radically this ride would change me and the way I move energy around my body on a daily basis.

So many of my days in the past would begin with a scan of emails or a scroll of social media on my phone, seeing things that would cause me a little stress and anxiety. I'd rush around getting ready, eager to message people back or answer queries. The reason this used to cause such panic in me is that I didn't want customers to think that I was ignoring their emails or being unresponsive.

By the time I actually got to sit down at my laptop, my heart would be racing, thinking about all that I had to do that day, including answering all the messages that I'd received overnight.

Because of this anxiety, my mornings would set me up in the wrong way and all those anxious thoughts would be the undercurrent spoiling my day.

Once I discovered EFT, all of this changed.

EFT can be a transformative tool in our lives. The influence of our emotional states on our reality cannot be overstated. While joy, love and excitement can attract abundance and success, lingering negative emotions like fear, anxiety and doubt often manifest more of the same challenges, keeping us trapped in cycles that hinder our progress and well-being.

Imagine living your life unaware of the power that your emotions wield over your reality.

Consider how the unchecked flow of negativity could influence your life's outcomes, possibly leading you down paths that diverge from your desired destiny. The absence of tools like EFT in your personal care arsenal could mean missed opportunities for healing, growth and achieving your true potential.

EFT offers more than just temporary relief. It provides a pathway to lasting change by addressing the root causes of emotional distress. The process not only clears the way for enhanced emotional equilibrium but also paves the path for heightened manifestations in all aspects of life.

But what happens if we continue on without harnessing such a powerful tool? Life without the knowledge and application of EFT might mean remaining in the dark about the underlying causes of our emotional upheavals. It could result in prolonged suffering from issues that could have been resolved or mitigated. The potential for personal growth and achievement could be stifled, leaving us feeling unfulfilled and disconnected from our true selves and our ability to manifest our desires effectively.

Consider how its integration into your daily routine could transform not just your emotional health but your entire life. The journey of self-discovery and healing is about moving towards a life filled with joy, abundance and peace. It's about turning the ordinary into the extraordinary and realising that within you lies the power to change your world.

We need to step forward with the willingness to explore, understand and utilise this easy tool to see where this journey of healing and transformation can take us.

The Practical Application of EFT

Think of EFT as a way to erase negative thoughts, similar to using a remote control to switch channels. This method helps you shift your focus and emotions from problems and anxiety to positivity and calm, much like how changing the channel changes your entire viewing experience.

Each session allows you to detach these burdensome thoughts and replace them with positive affirmations – reconfiguring the entire train of your thought process towards a more positive direction. Over time, this train, once laden with negativity, begins to brighten as these positive affirmations take root.

EFT isn't just a reactive technique. It can be a proactive daily practice, too. Initiating your day with a tapping session can set a tone of positivity and resilience. Likewise, concluding the day with EFT can help decompress and prepare for restful sleep, allowing the subconscious processes to integrate the day's positive affirmations. The ripple effects of EFT extend beyond personal tranquillity. As my inner narrative evolved, so too did my external interactions. Relationships deepened, opportunities that previously seemed formidable became attainable and life's colours appeared more vivid and engaging.

EFT's transformative power isn't just anecdotal either. It's supported by numerous personal testimonies. For instance, a client of mine once shared how EFT helped her overcome a longstanding phobia of water that not only affected her ability to enjoy leisure activities but also impeded all of her time abroad on holiday when she would visit the beach.

Through regular tapping sessions focused on her fears and self-acceptance, she was not only able to overcome her fears but even came to love swimming lessons with her daughter!

Breaking Down Barriers

In 2021, my journey with EFT began under a cloud of scepticism. The concept of tapping various body points while reciting affirmations seemed too far-fetched for me – too "woo-woo", even. The first time I tried it, I had thoughts of, "What the heck am I doing here?" as I frantically tapped on points across my body. "How is this helping me?" I thought.

I had so many questions. How could such a simple technique address the complex layers of emotions like anxiety or grief that I wrestled with? And if it really did work, why have I never heard anyone talk about it? Why isn't it taught in school?

But once I started to feel the benefits, my thought process around all of this changed, and one of the beautiful things about EFT is that you see instant results!

Those results are subtle yet deep. In my case, there was a noticeable shift in my mood and a decrease in the physical tension that I carried in my body. This initial change sparked my curiosity and led me to delve deeper into the practice. Each tapping session seemed to peel away layers of stress and anxiety, revealing a calmer version of myself underneath.

It wasn't long before I started incorporating EFT into my daily routine, using it as a tool to combat the everyday stresses of life.

This fresh belief I had in the power of EFT inspired me to learn more about its methodology and the science behind it. As I educated myself, I felt a growing responsibility to share this knowledge. The lack of widespread awareness and the scepticism surrounding EFT motivated me to become an advocate for its benefits. I began by sharing my experiences with friends and family, guiding them through the basics of tapping and watching as they, too, experienced its immediate benefits.

The more I shared, the more feedback I received about the positive impacts of EFT on others' lives. Friends reported better sleep, reduced anxiety and even improvements in physical pain conditions. These testimonials fuelled my passion and led me to host workshops and group sessions online, spreading the word about EFT's potential more broadly.

EFT is more than just a personal healing tool – it's a scientifically grounded approach that can significantly enhance both emotional and physical well-being. To truly appreciate the effectiveness of EFT, it's essential to understand its basis in both psychology and physiology.

Psychological Foundations of EFT

EFT works on the principle that our thoughts and emotions aren't just transient feelings but neurochemical processes that can have huge effects on our mental health and bodily functions. When we experience negative emotions, our brain releases specific hormones and neurotransmitters that can affect everything from our mood to our immune response. EFT helps interrupt these neurochemical processes by targeting the source of the emotional disturbance.

Through the process of tapping on specific meridian points on the body, EFT sends signals directly to the amygdala and other parts of the brain involved in controlling emotion and fear. These signals help to calm the mind, reduce stress and anxiety and promote a state of emotional balance.

This is similar to rebooting your body's system, encouraging a shift from a stress-induced fight-or-flight response to a more relaxed rest-and-digest state, which is essential for healing and health.

Physiological Impacts of EFT

On a physiological level, tapping on meridian points improves the flow of energy and removes blockages in the body's bioenergy system. Doing so alleviates physical pain and contributes to better health and vitality. The stimulation of these points can also improve blood circulation, reduce muscle tension, and foster hormone balance, which can have wide-ranging health benefits from improved sleep patterns to enhanced digestion.

These physiological changes are crucial for long-term health and well-being, as they help the body maintain its natural balance and promote self-healing. The simplicity of EFT, combined with its immediate effects on the body's energy system, make it a potent tool for health maintenance and disease prevention.

The Universal Appeal of EFT

The universal nature of EFT lies in the simplicity and immediacy of its effects.

It's a tool that can be easily learned and applied by anyone, from children in schools learning how to manage their stress and anxieties to adults dealing with complex emotional traumas or physical illnesses. Healthcare professionals around the world are beginning to recognise the benefits of EFT and are integrating it into treatment plans as a complementary therapy.

By fostering an understanding of the psychological and physiological bases of EFT, we can demystify this practice and enhance its acceptance in mainstream healthcare. This acceptance could transform EFT into a widely used tool across various settings, helping us manage our emotional and physical health with a simple yet effective, approach.

Understanding EFT

EFT merges cognitive psychology's principles with acupressure's ancient science. It involves tapping on specific meridian points on the body in a defined sequence, each linked to traditional Chinese medicine pathways believed to regulate emotional health. This physical interaction, coupled with verbal positive affirmations, aims to recalibrate the mind's response to emotional stress, effectively "rewiring" the brain's conditioned reactions.

After a shoulder injury in the gym in 2020, I was having a sports massage by my friend Josie, when she suddenly told me to lay still and not move a muscle.

I was face down when I started feeling little tingling sensations across my back and shoulders. She had started putting little acupuncture needles into my skin. Within a few minutes, a sensation of peace, calm and clarity washed across my entire body. I'd heard of acupuncture before, but the needles always put me off to be quite honest. Josie was desperate for me to try it and feel the benefits first-hand. (She's trained.)

Acupuncture concentrates on popping needles into each of the body's meridian points. The function of meridians is to transport life energy, connect the organs, communicate between the internal and external parts of the body, and distribute fluids and essence. Any blockage, deficiency, or excess of energy in the meridians can lead to physical, mental or emotional ill health.

Tapping is much less invasive as no needles are required, but we all have meridian lines across our bodies. In EFT, tapping on these meridian points is used to release energy blockages that can cause negative emotions and physical symptoms.

In one of my very first EFT sessions, which centred on alleviating anxiety around public speaking, the facilitator guided us all through a sequence of tapping points while we repeated, "Even though I feel nervous about speaking, I deeply and completely love and accept myself." The only public speaking I had done at that point was in the NHS to around 100 people when we launched a website for mental health users. I stood there, hiding behind a podium, shaking like a leaf, and my 15-minute introductory speech turned into around three minutes of drivel!

However, in this EFT session, with each round of tapping, I felt that harsh grip of anxiety loosen. By the time the session came to an end, I was more participative; I also noticed a genuine shift in my attitude toward public speaking.

I felt like I could stand on a stage and present a talk to thousands of people.

But how did it work internally? And how did I feel such a shift in my mindset almost instantly?

Using EFT to Remove Limiting Beliefs

With all of this information in hand, I decided to see if EFT could be used to retrain all the negative thoughts we had about our limiting beliefs. Why wouldn't it? After all, these are just the deep-seated convictions that constrain our potential and impact our thoughts, behaviours, and the outcomes of our lives!

The first step in EFT involves identifying specific limiting beliefs that you want to change. These beliefs might be about self-worth, capabilities or possibilities in life, such as "I'm not good enough", "I can't succeed in business", or "I don't deserve happiness." EFT starts with the acknowledgement of these beliefs, which is crucial because recognising and articulating the belief is the first step towards changing it.

For example, consider someone who struggles with a limiting belief related to their professional capabilities, such as "I'm not competent enough to lead projects." This belief could prevent them from seeking leadership roles or asserting their ideas during team meetings.

By using EFT, you could specifically target and tap on this negative belief while simultaneously affirming, "Even though I feel uncertain about my ability to lead, I deeply and completely love and accept myself and trust in my capabilities."

During the tapping sessions, focus on points that stimulate feelings of self-confidence and calm. This process can help lessen the emotional weight of self-doubt and gradually instil a sense of confidence.

Over time, as the sessions continue, the belief of not being capable enough can be replaced by a more empowering belief, such as "I'm skilled and capable of leading projects successfully." This change in mindset could encourage you to volunteer for leadership opportunities, participate more actively in discussions, or even showcase your potential in professional settings.

Whilst tapping, we're encouraged to verbalise our limiting beliefs in a specific format, starting with acknowledgement and moving towards a more positive or neutral reframing.

For instance, we might say, "Even though I believe I'm not good enough, I deeply and completely love and accept myself." This helps in consciously acknowledging the beliefs whilst also promoting a self-accepting attitude critical for personal growth.

Once the emotional intensity of the limiting belief is reduced, EFT focuses on instilling new, positive beliefs. This is done through affirmations that are repeated during the tapping sessions.

For instance, after addressing fears of inadequacy, we might tap while repeating, "I am capable and competent." This practice helps to embed these positive affirmations into the subconscious, making them a part of our automatic thought patterns.

Changing deep-seated beliefs isn't a one-time effort. In fact, like most other techniques, it requires consistency. Repeated EFT sessions help to reinforce the new positive beliefs and gradually overwrite the old limiting ones.

Each session helps to weaken the hold of negative beliefs and strengthen the presence of empowering ones. Each session need only be three to five minutes; I'm not talking hours at a time. I sometimes even do it in short, sharp bursts: a few seconds whilst sat at traffic lights on my way to a meeting, a few seconds whilst cooking on an evening at home, a few seconds whilst brushing my teeth. It all mounts up, and the more frequent we are with doing it, the better our response will be to it.

As the limiting beliefs are dismantled, there's often a noticeable change in emotions and behaviours. We might feel more confident, less anxious and more open to opportunities.

Behaviourally, we might take on challenges we would have previously avoided or engage in social interactions more freely, demonstrating the incredible impact of changing our belief system through EFT.

Building Resilience Against Setbacks

The path to achieving our goals through manifestation is rarely a straight line. It often involves navigating a series of ups and downs, successes and setbacks. The ability to bounce back from these setbacks, often referred to as resilience, is crucial for long-term success in any endeavour, including manifestation. EFT can be a powerful tool in building this essential resilience, helping us to manage disappointment and maintain our focus and motivation despite challenges.

In terms of manifestation, setbacks can take many forms – whether it's a goal that takes longer to achieve than expected, unexpected obstacles, or outcomes that don't align with our desires. These setbacks can be discouraging and may lead to doubts about our abilities and the effectiveness of our manifesting efforts. Such negative emotions, if not managed properly, can create a cycle of negativity that hinders further progress.

EFT simply provides a method for addressing the emotional impact of setbacks in a structured way, allowing us to release negative emotions associated with these challenges and reinforce our commitment to our goals.

It helps in quickly addressing emotions like frustration, disappointment, or anger that often accompany setbacks. By tapping on specific meridian points and focusing on these emotions, we can effectively reduce our intensity, clearing the way for more constructive emotions and responses. EFT additionally allows us to reframe our perspective on these setbacks.

Instead of viewing them as failures, tapping sessions can help us see them as opportunities for learning and growth. This reframing is reinforced through affirmations integrated into the tapping routine such as "every setback is a setup for a comeback" or "I learn and grow from every challenge."

After reducing the negative emotional load, EFT focuses on boosting positive beliefs and determination. For instance, affirmations like "I am resilient and persistent" and "I stay focused on my goals, regardless of obstacles" can be tapped into the subconscious, strengthening our resilience. By clearing out negative emotions and reinforcing positive intentions, EFT helps maintain focus and motivation.

This is essential in manifestation, as sustained effort and a positive outlook are key drivers of success. After a setback, I turn to EFT immediately. A quick tapping session can really help me manage that initial emotional response and prevent it from escalating any further.

Tapping Into a Wealthy Lifestyle

When I first joined Denise Duffield-Thomas' Money Bootcamp membership, her one-hour live calls would always end in a round of tapping.

She'd ask us to get comfortable, close our eyes, and bring any of our thoughts about money being hard to come by to the forefront of our minds, almost to the point that we felt consumed in that stomach-churning emotion of never having enough.

Once we connected with that energy internally, Denise would ask us to tap, repeating statements such as "Even though money is hard to come by, even though I'll never have enough, even though bills are aplenty, even though I find it hard to make money online, I deeply and completely love and accept myself." We'd then go into rounds of tapping in positive affirmations stating the opposite of these beliefs, and by the end of the session, I'd leave the call feeling like I could take on the world!

One of the best things about tapping is that you can create your own scripts. So, I crafted myself a few rounds of tapping, including statements that really triggered my own thoughts in relation to financial wealth. I'd tap on these feelings, stirring up all the emotions inside, before thrashing them with statements of positivity, and most days after doing so, I'd have a little brainwave about what I could do in my business to bring about more abundance and success.

Was this coincidental? To you, maybe! As for me, I don't believe in coincidence.

I believe that everything has meaning and that everything happens for a reason. It almost felt like I was awakening dormant thoughts within myself that had always been there, I just needed that tapping session to give them life.

After crafting my own wealth scripts, my money mindset changed drastically. Since doing this on a daily basis, I now consistently turnover £30k a month with my business, and I truly believe that I can achieve anything, whereas previously I was placing blocks and limiting beliefs upon myself in that area specifically.

As we become more adept at recognising and addressing our internal blockages with EFT, we often find that not only do our original goals become more attainable, but we also feel more empowered to set and achieve even higher aspirations. Only recently have I adapted my scripts to hit £60k per month.

And guess how much I turned over in business just last month?

£59,940!

Need I say more?

By integrating EFT into regular self-care routines, we can maintain a clearer path to success, free from the unseen obstacles that once hindered our progress. This ongoing practice helps ensure that the path to achieving our full potential is as unobstructed as possible, allowing for continual growth and accomplishment.

Integrating EFT Into Our Lives

Each morning for me now begins not with the blare of an alarm, but with a quiet moment of tapping. Before the day's demands sweep me away, I sit by my bedside and start my tapping routine, focusing on setting a positive intention for the day – I sometimes do it whilst showering.

For example, if I've got a challenging meeting coming up, it can start to stir up mixed emotions for me. I'd feel excited about it, but at the same time, I know I shy away from difficult conversations, so my anxiety would more than likely come out on top!

I tap on my facial meridian points whilst affirming, "Even though I feel anxious about this meeting, I deeply and completely love and accept myself and instead choose to feel calm and confident." This practice helps alleviate my morning anxiety and empowers me to approach my day with a grounded and centred presence.

Like many of you reading this, I often face a slump in energy and focus around midday. This was extremely prevalent when I worked in the NHS, which is why I always booked meetings in the morning to get them out of the way. I'd usually need a little pick-me-up at lunchtime to prepare me for the long afternoon slog.

Instead of reaching for a cup of coffee now, I turn to EFT to rejuvenate my mental clarity.

During a quick break, I'll tap on my meridian points whilst focusing on affirmations like, "I am filled with energy and focus." This invigorates both my physical and mental states, allowing me to tackle the afternoon with renewed strength. This simple five-minute routine can dramatically shift the trajectory of my day.

EFT is particularly effective for managing unexpected stressors. For instance, back in 2021, I was having my website redesigned by a company. They told me everything was ready to go, and so I announced to all of my followers about this new and exciting website facelift.

When I was actually shown the website, I hated it. It just wasn't me. It was bland, hard to find anything, and just generally looked awful. I was told that to redesign it they would need a further four to six weeks, and so, true to form, my initial reaction was frustration and anxiety.

Instead of letting these feelings spiral, I engaged in a focused tapping session after the meeting, using affirmations such as "I choose to respond with calmness and find productive solutions." This immediate application of EFT helped me go back to the company with my thoughts and return to the situation with a solution-oriented mindset, significantly altering my interaction with the team and the project's outcome.

Ending the day with EFT helps me to unwind and process the day's events. This practice involves tapping on any residual stress from the day and affirming positive reflections, such as, "I release the day's worries and am grateful for its joys and lessons." This not only aids in emotional decompression but also promotes better sleep, setting a restorative tone for the night ahead.

Those are just a few examples of how I use EFT in my daily life. EFT isn't only for daily fluctuations, however. It also allows us to shine during life's significant events. For example, when I was preparing for a major personal milestone – the launch of my online Academy – I was really nervous to put myself out there as a tutor and coach, and I had so many feelings of worry about being judged by others.

I used EFT extensively to manage overwhelming emotions and stress. Tapping on my fears and anxieties about the big launch helped me remain present and enjoy one of the most important events in my business fully.

Integrating EFT into daily life doesn't require monumental changes to your routine. Instead, it's about incorporating small, manageable sessions that collectively lead to significant emotional and psychological benefits. Each tapping session builds on the last, creating a cumulative effect that enhances overall well-being.

My hope is that by sharing these examples from my life, you too can see the practicality and huge impact of EFT.

Whether you're dealing with daily stressors, seeking to enhance your personal productivity, or navigating major life events, EFT offers a versatile and powerful tool to improve your emotional health and overall quality of life.

Activity

To enhance your experience and provide you with practical tools to tackle those pesky limiting beliefs, I've created a comprehensive tapping guide and an accompanying video, available exclusively for you.

You can download these free resources at cannycrystalsacademy. co.uk/limitless. This guide will introduce you to the fundamentals of EFT.

The video demonstrates the tapping techniques step-by-step, making it easy for you to follow along and apply the methods to your own situations. Whether you're new to tapping or looking to deepen your practice, these resources are designed to assist you in effectively dissolving your limiting beliefs.

Try incorporating tapping into your daily routine and observe how your negative beliefs begin to shift, day by day, paving the way for a more empowered life.

Chapter 11
Alignment Through the Balance of Energy

I'd like you to think about the role of a gardener, each day tending to a vibrant and colourful garden. Every flower and every plant there represents different aspects of your life, each requiring specific attention and care to thrive.

Just as a well-balanced ecosystem in a garden promotes healthy plant life, well-balanced energy in our lives encourages health and well-being. This balance is what practises like Reiki and Feng Shui aim to achieve, acting like tools that help us tend to and nurture our personal living spaces – both within our minds and in our physical environments.

Discovering Energy

My first experience of energy healing was at a local spiritualist church. I was born and raised in a little mining village just outside of Durham and my mam and aunties were always dragging me to Sunday school and Christian evenings at a

Methodist church. I've always hated being forced into doing things; my natural instinct was to rebel.

When I hit the age of 16, one of my best friends told me about a spiritualist church just up the road from where we lived. After looking into it, I saw that they were putting on a healing night, whereby you could attend for an hour and someone would heal whatever part of your body needed that renewal.

I remember turning up to it on my own thinking it would be packed. As I walked in, I was greeted by two little old women just sitting having a chat amongst themselves. They welcomed me with open arms, then a cup of tea and some biscuits. Afterward, they asked why I was there.

At the time, I had just recently broken up with my then-long-term partner, and I was in absolute bits internally. I didn't want to give too much away to the two little old ladies, so I just told them I was feeling lost and stuck in life, and that I needed a bit of general healing.

One of them took me to the very front of the Church and sat me on a chair, telling me to sit comfortably with my hands on my knees and take a few deep breaths. On the last one, she told me to close my eyes and relax, and she would let me know once she was finished.

I couldn't keep my eyes closed because I'm naturally a nosey person. I started peeping every now and again through squinted eyes, and there she was, this little old lady, using her hands to scan over my body, not touching me, maybe an inch or two away from my body. When I had my eyes closed, it was almost like I could feel the warmth coming from her hands. If you rub both of your hands together, you get a heated friction feeling, and that is what this felt like.

I remember closing my eyes fully once I had seen this and I just let her get on with it.

After about 30 minutes of silence, I opened my eyes and it appeared that she was sat in a trance – her hands were in front of me, palms facing towards me, circling around the centre of my chest. I remember being startled when she suddenly spoke.

She said something along the lines of, "Your heart is such a mess" – it was crazy that she had picked up on how heartbroken I was at the time. She said that she had done her best, but the energy in and around my heart was too out of place.

I thanked her for whatever she had done, and as I stood up to leave, I felt a sense of contentment wash over my entire being.

I suddenly felt lighter, and that the problems I entered the church with were different from those I was leaving with. It was almost like someone had turned a light on inside of me, illuminating the different parts of my mind that I'd previously kept in the dark.

I vividly remember that night having the best night's sleep, and waking up the next morning without a care in the world, and honestly, I never looked back on the relationship that I had left.

It was such a positive experience for me.

And it wasn't until I started going through my spiritual journey and looking into alternative therapies like Reiki that I realised that's exactly what that was.

The Energy of Reiki

At the start of 2020, I remember seeing an advert on Groupon or Wowcher, one of those voucher sites, for a one-hour Reiki session for just £15. Amidst the depths of the Coronavirus pandemic, like most people, I was feeling a little deflated. I was entrenched in both physical and emotional discomfort.

I started doing research into what Reiki was. It's a healing technique developed in Japan in the early 20th century. This introduced me to the concept of manipulating the subtle energies that flow through our bodies, much like the way our metaphorical gardener channels water to nourish those plants. Sceptical, yet desperate, I decided to take the leap and attended my first session.

Picture this: There I was in this random lady's back garden in a custom-made shed, lying on a massage bench with meditative music on! I vaguely remember thinking, "Mart, what are you doing now?"

As Heather, the Reiki Master, explained what the session would entail, I felt comforted as I kind of knew what to expect, as well as knowing a lot more about Reiki itself from my extensive research. Heather had me wear a blindfold so that I could fully concentrate, focus, and switch off from any external disturbances.

As I lay there on the bed, I felt the strangest of feelings.

At one point, I could have sworn she had held onto my feet, stroking my legs, but then I could hear her footsteps behind my shoulders at the top of the bed. I was so confused. It was almost like my other senses had gone into overdrive: I was picking up on the smallest of things around my energy field.

Because I had the blindfold on, I also began seeing weird things. At one point, clear as day, I saw my grandma's grave. I have no idea why this image popped up in my mind so clearly, but I acknowledged it and let it pass. It was similar to seeing clouds passing by in front of my face, each one depicted with a visual sign.

The next thing I saw was myself in front of a live TV audience – I was sitting on a couch, someone was interviewing me, and people were staring back at me, hanging on my every word.

At one point, I even had a vision of my mam just cutting up vegetables in her kitchen! I can't explain what I saw. It was so surreal.

After being laid there for what seemed like a few short minutes, my physical body started acting weird and began jolting, as though I was being electrocuted. It did it three times in total over the hour session, and I remember my Apple Watch vibrating in unison whenever my body had this reaction.

You know when you have those dreams that you've stepped off a curb or fallen from a building, and you immediately jolt up in bed? That was the same sensation as what I experienced.

After an hour into the session, Heather started to get me visualising grounding myself to safely bring my consciousness back to reality. I saw my energetic body growing roots from every contact point, plunging deeper and deeper into the Earth's core. The roots eventually turned golden, shimmering as they solidified in my visualisation.

I slowly began to sit upright in my physical body, removing my blindfold in the process. I looked at my watch, thinking someone had been trying to contact me with the constant vibrations and was shocked at what I saw.

The reason it had been vibrating was that it was detecting an unusually low heart rate.

My heart rate had dropped to about 40 beats per minute. I guess that was because I was in such a trance-like state, chilled and relaxed throughout the session.

When I asked Heather if the jolting throughout was normal, she said that it had happened before with other clients. According to her, it's usually the energy inside of our bodies shifting itself around and rearranging.

I was fascinated!

It was such a strange feeling and one I'll never forget.

I remember driving home afterwards and feeling so alert, so alive, with the willpower that I could achieve anything.

The next day, I was up at the crack of dawn, and even took myself off for a swim before work! I had such a productive week in terms of life itself. It was as though the Reiki had healed my entire body from the inside out, almost like a switch had been flipped inside me, illuminating my internal landscape with energy and vitality.

The Principles and Benefits of Reiki

Reiki offers an avenue for enhancing personal well-being through the management of life force energy known as "Qi" or "Ki." Practised through gentle, non-invasive hand placements, Reiki practitioners channel that universal energy to the recipient, aiming to enhance the body's natural healing processes and restore balance, both physically and emotionally.

Engaging in Reiki sessions can lead to a whole host of benefits. Just like in my experience, stress reduction and relaxation are among the most immediate effects, with many people feeling a significant release of tension after just one session. This relaxation response can also promote better sleep patterns, which is crucial for overall health and well-being.

Reiki goes beyond mere relaxation though. It also promotes healing.

By restoring the balance of energy in the body, Reiki can alleviate pain, support immune system function, and aid in the recovery process from illness and injury. It's also been linked to enhancing mental clarity and emotional stability, allowing us to handle daily stresses with greater calmness and resilience.

Reiki is also used as a complementary therapy alongside conventional medical treatments. It can help lessen side effects, reduce pain, and improve the recovery rate from surgical and long-term illnesses. It provides the emotional support necessary for recovery, helping patients handle the psychological burdens of their conditions. The relaxation effect of Reiki can often help improve sleep. Better sleep leads to a range of benefits for the body, including improved immune function, reduced inflammation and a better mood.

Opting out of Reiki won't lead to direct negative consequences; however, bypassing its benefits can mean that you'd be missing out on a holistic tool that could complement other health efforts.

Without Reiki, I might have found myself relying solely on more conventional practices to heal my heartache that addresses primarily physical symptoms, potentially overlooking the emotional and energetic dimensions of health that Reiki targets.

Incorporating Reiki into your wellness routine isn't just about dealing with existing health issues. It's about proactive self-care. It offers a way to maintain balance in your life, promote ongoing health, and foster an inner sense of peace that's valuable in our busy lives. Engaging with its practices can significantly enhance your quality of life, providing a valuable complement to other health and wellness practices mentioned in this book.

Reiki is grounded in the belief that everyone has a life force energy that flows through us and is what causes us to be alive. If our life force energy is low, then we're more likely to get sick or feel stressed. And if it's high, we're more capable of being happy and healthy.

The core of Reiki is guided by the five Reiki principles, which were introduced by Mikao Usui as a way to promote a healthy way of living:

> "Just for today, I will not be angry.
>
> Just for today, I will not worry.
>
> Just for today, I will be grateful.
>
> Just for today, I will do my work honestly.
>
> Just for today, I will be kind to every living thing."

Reiki helps to promote balance on all levels – physical, mental, and emotional. It works directly to restore balance in the energetic system of the body. It can also help spiritually, although Reiki is not tied to any religion or spiritual practice. Many find that it brings a greater sense of inner peace and harmony, which can be valuable in today's often chaotic world.

Regular Reiki treatments can also bring about a calmer and more peaceful state of being, in which a person would be better able to cope with everyday stress. This mental balance also enhances learning, memory, and mental clarity. In such a state, we can then make better decisions and improve our quality of life.

Reiki healing quickly returns you to your natural state. At the least, it gets your body moving in the right direction. That means your breathing, heart rate, blood pressure, circulation, and other bodily systems improve. As your physical body improves, so does your emotional health and wellness.

It can relieve pain from migraine, arthritis, sciatica and menopause, to name a few. It also helps with symptoms of asthma, chronic fatigue and insomnia.

You don't need to be into spirituality to enjoy the benefits of Reiki. However, for many people, Reiki opens the doors to a greater understanding of the Universe and their own spirituality. It can help clear emotions, leading to a strengthened sense of self and happiness.

Though Reiki isn't a cure for a disease or illness, it may assist the body in creating an environment to facilitate that healing. Reiki is a great tool to use as a complement to traditional medicine and is practised in many hospitals and medical care settings.

Many people find that using Reiki enables them to live their lives more fully by helping them manage their stress levels more effectively or by giving them more energy. They come to realise that they have a role in keeping themselves healthy and that balancing their systems can help them feel more alive, relaxed and full of enthusiasm.

Encountering Reiki is like discovering a hidden inner reservoir of healing energy – a wellspring of health and vitality that rejuvenates and brings wellness to every aspect of life.

The Journey to Becoming a Reiki Healer

Motivated by the initial effects of Reiki on myself, I went on a huge spiritual journey to delve deeper into this practice. I learned about the body's energy centres, known as chakras, and how Reiki seeks to align and balance these centres to promote health and well-being. Each level of Reiki training opened new dimensions of understanding about how energy affects our physical and emotional health and how we can consciously manipulate this energy to heal ourselves and others.

As I progressed through my course, I began to apply Reiki to myself regularly, using it as a tool to maintain my energy balance, much like how our gardener routinely waters, prunes and tends to plants.

Regular practice significantly enhanced my sensitivity to the energies around me, enriching my interactions with others and deepening my connection to the world while keeping me grounded.

To this day, I use Reiki on my crystals to supercharge them with energy, on my affirmation candles before lighting them to empower my visualisations, and even sometimes on my dog, JJ, when I feel like he needs a little bit of internal healing.

Harmonising My Environment

In parallel with my Reiki journey, I started to think about the energy of everything around me, including the items in my home, my office and everything I came into contact with on a daily basis.

My extensive research led me to start exploring Feng Shui, the ancient Chinese art of placement. Feng Shui taught me to see my living space as a garden of energy, where the arrangement of space could influence the flow and quality of the energy within it. I learned to arrange furniture, decorations and even colours in ways that enhanced the flow of positive energy whilst minimising negativity.

Feng Shui was developed over 3,000 years ago and is a complex body of knowledge that reveals how to balance the energies of any given space to assure health and good fortune for the people inhabiting it.

The phrase "Feng Shui" literally translates as "wind-water" in English, which is a nod to its origins in ancient Chinese astronomy and the belief in the influence of the stars on the Earth.

The practice involves arranging your living or working spaces in ways that align with natural energy flows, which are believed to impact the environment's Qi, or life force, similar to Reiki.

Back in 2022, I reached out to Kimberley, a Feng Shui consultant, and she mapped my home according to the Bagua, even detailing the colours and elements I should have present in each room.

Upon reading Kimberley's report of my house, I immediately got in my car and went to the closest B&M Bargains to pick up some supplies. My home was apparently in need of colours that represented the fire element in most spaces, so I picked up a fruit bowl to fill with red apples and oranges, some red candle jars and a couple of burnt orange cushions to strategically place.

She also mentioned that the energy comes in through the front door of the home and leaves via the back door.

We live in a house where, as soon as you come in via the front entrance, you can see straight through to the patio doors (what's known as a "shotgun home"), and so to expand the energy flow and ensure it actually meanders through the house, I should place something to disperse the energy, such as a chandelier, or a plant... and so I bought both for the entrance to our home!

Once home, I started implementing her recommendations, or as she referred to them, remedies.

Kimberley advised that I close all the plug holes in our bathrooms and kitchen, as well as all toilet seats, to stop the energy escaping.

I must have looked crazy as I explained to Jonny that we're now keeping them all closed to improve our health and wealth. To be honest, this must have been the hardest part; bringing him on board to police the Feng Shui in the house and to not touch all the random bowls of sea shells, pieces of fruit, and plates of metal strategically placed across the home.

Since putting these remedies into place, the energy within our house has really changed: The quality of our sleep has got a lot better, wealth flows effortlessly to us, the conversations we have are more productive and meaningful, and overall, there's a harmonious vibe that just seems to permeate every corner of our home.

It's almost as if by arranging our environment to facilitate the optimal flow of energy, we've attuned to a frequency that promotes prosperity, wellness and happiness.

Kimberley's guidance helped me see our home not just as a physical space but as a living entity, where every element and every corner has a purpose and an impact on our lives. The strategic placement of colour, elements, and objects according to Feng Shui principles has transformed our living space into a catalyst for positive change.

It's fascinating how these ancient practices, when applied thoughtfully, can yield such gigantic modern benefits.

The journey didn't stop with just a few changes.

Over the months, I continued to tweak and adjust our arrangements as we grew more attuned to the needs of our space and its effects on our lives. Each small change seemed to bring with it a fresh wave of positive energy, encouraging me to delve even deeper into the world of Feng Shui.

It's a testament to the power of our environment to shape our health, our wealth and our relationships.

For anyone sceptical about the impacts of such an ancient practice in today's modern world, I invite you to explore Feng Shui for yourselves. You might just find, as I did, that your space holds the key to enhancing your life's energy and unlocking your full potential.

The Principles and Benefits of Feng Shui

Feng Shui operates on several principles:

The five elements theory. This involves wood, fire, earth, metal, and water, and how their interactions affect balance and harmony in our environment.

The Bagua. An energy map that divides any given space into nine areas, each corresponding to different life aspects such as wealth, health, career, and love.

Yin and Yang. This principle is centred on creating balance and harmony through opposing forces, such as black and white, light and dark. It's crucial for ensuring energy flows smoothly without disruption.

Feng Shui helps in arranging a living environment that promotes well-being. By following its principles, we can create a space that strengthens health, beckons wealth, and fosters loving relationships, all of which contribute to our overall happiness.

By organising a workspace according to Feng Shui, you can enhance clarity, focus, and productivity. The placement of your desk, the direction you face while working, and the organisation of your office can significantly influence your effectiveness and career success.

Feng Shui can influence personal energy by dictating the flow of Qi in the environments where we live and work. A well-arranged home using Feng Shui can lead to a rejuvenating and energising atmosphere, whilst poor Feng Shui can lead to lethargy and negativity.

Practising Feng Shui principles can improve your health by helping to create a more balanced living environment. It considers factors such as air quality, light and flow, which all significantly impact your health.

Specific areas of your home are linked to wealth according to the Bagua map. By enhancing these areas with appropriate Feng Shui adjustments, you can potentially increase your wealth. This might include adding elements that represent abundance and wealth, such as plants that symbolise growth, water features that signify the flow of money, or mirrors that double positive energy.

Feng Shui can also be applied to foster better relationships and a vibrant social life. The arrangement of the living spaces can affect personal interactions. For instance, creating a welcoming and comfortable environment in the home can encourage positive interactions among family members and guests.

In the hustle and bustle of life, one of the most significant benefits Feng Shui offers is creating a peaceful, quiet and comforting home environment where we can escape the stresses of everyday life. The proper arrangement according to Feng Shui can transform a chaotic home into a peaceful sanctuary.

Feng Shui is much more than just a way of arranging your living spaces. It's a philosophy that can help you to live a more deliberate and intentional life. By understanding and manipulating the energies within your environment, you can enhance your well-being and live your best possible life.

Whether it's through the strategic placement of furniture, the use of specific colours or the incorporation of natural elements, Feng Shui offers practical and mystical avenues to improve every aspect of your existence, harmonising your personal environment with your inner life to create peace, stability and happiness.

The Combined Impact on My Life

The integration of Reiki and Feng Shui in my daily life cultivated a profound harmonisation between my internal state and my external surroundings. By channelling Reiki energy to align and balance my body's energy centres and arranging my living space according to Feng Shui principles to optimise the flow of Qi, I created a dynamic synergy that bolstered my overall wellness.

This harmonious balance had a tangible impact on my physical and mental health. Regular Reiki sessions helped alleviate chronic stress and minor bodily pains, enhancing my physical health and allowing my body to rejuvenate more effectively. Similarly, by employing Feng Shui techniques, such as positioning furniture to encourage positive energy flow and using colours that evoked tranquillity, I noticed a significant boost in my mental clarity and focus. My home transformed into a reflection of calmness and order, mirroring the balanced state I cultivated within myself.

My energy levels also saw a marked improvement. The gentle yet profound realignment of my internal energy through Reiki, combined with the strategic setup of my living environment, meant that fatigue became less frequent. I woke up feeling more refreshed and maintained higher levels of energy throughout the day.

This vitality allowed me to engage more fully with my tasks and hobbies, contributing to a richer, more productive daily routine.

The sense of peace and contentment that pervaded my life was unparalleled.

My home, reorganised to promote good energy flow, became a true sanctuary. It became a nurturing space where I could thrive, reflect, and grow. The calmness and balance achieved through these practices afforded me a perspective that life's challenges were manageable and temporary. This mindset was crucial in maintaining an overall sense of well-being and deep satisfaction with life.

In essence, the dual practice of Reiki and Feng Shui enriched my existence in every aspect. The careful cultivation of my environment and the mindful balancing of my personal energy converged to create an aesthetic and comforting living space that was deeply supportive of my spiritual and emotional growth. Each day became more fulfilling. The integration empowered me to thrive, vibrantly.

Now, I want you to pause and reflect on the potential within you, just waiting to be unlocked through the balanced flow of energy in your environments and within yourself.

When you align your personal spaces and internal energy with the universal currents that govern all life, you step into a stream of wellness and vitality that enhances every moment. This isn't merely about feeling better. It's about transforming your entire existence.

By integrating these ancient practices into your daily life, you do more than create a tranquil space. You activate a powerful catalyst for personal growth and actualisation.

What opportunities might you miss, and how might your life's potential diminish, if you choose to overlook the transformative power of aligning your energy?

Activity

To empower you in harmonising the energy of your living space, I've crafted a basic guide to Feng Shui, which you can access from the free resources at cannycrystalsacademy.co.uk/limitless.

This guide is designed to help you understand and apply the principles of Feng Shui to map your home for optimal energy flow.

In the guide, you'll find specific steps on how to identify the key areas of your home that impact your daily life and well-being, such as the wealth corner, health sector and love area. You'll learn how to use the Bagua map to align your living space with your aspirations.

Utilising this guide, you can create a more balanced and harmonious environment that supports your goals and improves your overall quality of life. Follow the steps outlined to adjust your space, attract positive energy and manifest the changes you wish to see in your life.

Chapter 12
Connecting with Nature for Spiritual Growth

O ur world today is so fast-paced and technology-driven. It's easy to become disconnected from the natural environment. Yet, nature holds an inherent power to heal. The sights, sounds and smells of the natural world ground us and bring us back to a state of balance and harmony. Scientific studies show that spending time in nature can reduce stress, improve our mood and enhance overall well-being[14]. Moreover, it's in nature that we can escape the noise and chaos of daily life and find a sanctuary where we can reflect, recharge and reconnect with our inner selves.

Let's think about trees for a second. (Stick with me.)

Trees are rooted deeply in the Earth, drawing sustenance from the rich soil whilst their branches sway gently in the wind as they reach upwards toward the warmth and light of the sun. Just as a tree finds its strength and stability through its connection to the

Earth and sky, we too can find balance and spiritual growth by reconnecting with nature.

Grounding and Its Benefits

Grounding, also known as earthing, is a practice that involves reconnecting with the Earth's natural energy. This can be achieved through simple techniques that help to centre and stabilise our energy, reducing stress and promoting overall well-being.

One of the simplest ways to ground yourself is by walking barefoot on natural surfaces such as grass, sand or soil. This direct contact with the Earth can help to balance your energy and improve your mood. This is because the Earth has a slightly negative charge due to the presence of free electrons. When you walk barefoot, your body comes into direct contact with these electrons, allowing them to flow into your body and stabilise its energies. Specifically, this helps to neutralise positively charged free radicals in your body, which are associated with inflammation and various health issues.

When I first heard about grounding, my first thought was, "Why do I need to get rid of inflammation in my body? I'm not inflamed anywhere!" However, I've since learned that inflammation is the root cause of many chronic diseases and pain conditions. Chronic inflammation can be a silent issue, not always presenting obvious symptoms, but still wreaking havoc on the body. It can lead to conditions like arthritis, heart disease, diabetes, and even contribute to mental health issues such as depression and anxiety.

Studies have also shown that grounding can improve sleep patterns by regulating cortisol levels, a hormone related to stress and sleep cycles. Regular grounding can enhance our immune function too, making the body more resilient to illnesses. I know personally that I feel more energised and less fatigued after spending time grounded throughout the day.

The Challenges We Face

Incorporating grounding practices into daily life can present several challenges, particularly for those living in urban environments or with busy schedules.

Our modern lifestyle contributes to this disconnect from the Earth's natural electrical field. Wearing rubber-soled shoes and living in buildings insulate us from the Earth's natural electrical field. This disconnection can contribute to creating a buildup of positive charge in our bodies, leaving us feeling ungrounded and out of balance. Urban living often means limited access to natural spaces, making it difficult to find suitable locations for grounding activities like walking barefoot on grass or soil. Additionally, the constant hustle and bustle of city life can make it hard to find that tranquillity needed for effective grounding.

However, there are practical solutions to these challenges. For instance, urban dwellers can seek out local parks or green spaces, however small, and make it a routine to visit them regularly. Spending even a few minutes in these natural settings can provide significant grounding benefits. Time constraints are another common hurdle. With demanding work schedules, family responsibilities and other commitments, finding time for grounding practices can seem daunting, and yet another activity to fit onto your already overloaded plate!

To overcome this, it's helpful to integrate grounding activities into daily routines. Simple practices like standing barefoot in the backyard whilst enjoying a morning coffee or taking a few minutes to sit under a tree during a lunch break can be super effective.

For those who find it difficult to engage in grounding activities due to the cold or inclement weather, there are still ways to stay connected to the Earth's energy. Indoor grounding solutions, such as using grounding mats or grounding crystals, can be highly effective. These products simulate the effects of direct contact with the Earth and can be easily incorporated into daily life.

Ultimately, whilst challenges exist, they're not impossible to overcome. By being creative and flexible, we can find ways to incorporate grounding practices into our lives regardless of our living situation or schedule. The key is to prioritise these practices and recognise their importance for physical and mental well-being, thereby making a conscious effort to integrate them into daily life.

Nature as a Catalyst for Spiritual Development

Nature isn't only a place of physical healing, but also a source of spiritual growth for us all. Many spiritual traditions emphasise the importance of connecting with the natural world around us to enhance our spiritual journeys. This is because ultimately, nature is a wellspring of inspiration. The intricate beauty of a flower, the majesty of a mountain or the rhythmic ebb and flow of the ocean can all evoke a sense of wonder and awe.

It's these moments of connection that can inspire deeper reflection and spiritual insight within us. Think about it. Nature provides an ideal backdrop for meditation and contemplation. Whether sitting quietly by a stream or practising a walking meditation in a forest, the natural world can help to deepen your meditation practice and foster a greater sense of inner peace.

The elements of nature – earth, water, fire and air – hold powerful symbolic and energetic qualities. Engaging with these elements can enhance your spiritual practices. For example, sitting by a fire can symbolise transformation and renewal, whilst immersing yourself in water can represent cleansing and purification. Incorporating nature into your spiritual rituals and ceremonies can enhance their power and significance. Creating a sacred space outdoors, using natural objects such as stones, feathers or flowers, and aligning your practices with the cycles of the moon and seasons can deepen your connection to the natural world and the rhythms of life.

Flower Power

If I ask you to think about what a hippie looks like, you might say "Someone with long hair, wearing tie-dyed clothes, sitting cross-legged with a peace sign in hand," or even refer to them as a "tree hugger."

This image is deeply ingrained in popular culture, often representing a laid-back, nature-loving individual who rejects all conventional norms. While this stereotype encapsulates a certain era and lifestyle, it can also overshadow the broader and more nuanced reality of people who practise mindfulness and connect with nature today.

The modern embodiment of these practices is far from the stereotypical image of the hippie and is more about integrating mindfulness and nature into everyday life for tangible mental and physical health benefits.

Today, the mindfulness and nature connection are embraced by a diverse range of individuals, from business professionals to athletes, and even students. These practices have been scientifically validated for their benefits, enhancing cognitive function and improving emotional well-being.

The stereotype of the hippie often implies a certain level of detachment from society's hustle and bustle, yet mindfulness and nature connection are actually about re-engaging with life in a more meaningful and present way. It's about finding balance and resilience amidst our busy lives, not retreating from them.

This shift from counter-cultural symbols to mainstream wellness strategies shows just how these practices have evolved and gained acceptance across various segments of society. By clinging to outdated stereotypes, we risk dismissing the profound and accessible benefits of mindfulness and nature connection. It's not about adopting a hippie lifestyle but about enhancing our overall quality of life through practices that ground us and foster well-being.

Whether that be through mindful meditation, barefoot walks in the park or simply taking a moment to breathe deeply and appreciate the natural world around us, these practices offer a practical and scientifically supported path to better health and happiness. Embracing these practices means acknowledging their value in promoting a balanced, grounded and enriched life, irrespective of lifestyle or appearance.

A Trip to the Beach

When I was younger, in the Summer holidays, my mam would quite often take me to a seaside near to where we lived called South Shields. We were fortunate to live only a 30-minute drive from the coastline, and it's such a beautiful, sandy beach. We'd walk through the gorgeous, green park, cross the road, take a shortcut through the fairground and amusements, run up the enormous sand dunes and try to be the first to be able to see the sea.

I'd take my bucket and spade, a picnic, often a cousin or a friend from the street I grew up on, and we'd spend hours there just playing on the sand and in the sea, exploring caves and running around like absolute lunatics!

I vividly remember each time on the way home, my mam would say something along the lines of, "You'll sleep well tonight with all that fresh sea air!" and right she was. I'd get home and crash for the afternoon, sometimes even having a little power nap on the way home in the car.

Similarly, whenever I go abroad in my adult years, if I've been to the beach, I'll sleep like a baby! For most of my life, I've always just thought it was the sea air knocking me out, but since learning about grounding, I've come to realise that it's actually the fact that I'm connecting with the Earth on an energetic and spiritual level.

All those years walking barefoot on the sand feeling the cool, wet grains between my toes, and immersing myself in the natural elements weren't just enjoyable pastimes but profound grounding experiences. This connection with the Earth provided a sense of calm and balance, significantly contributing to the deep, restorative sleep I experienced.

Understanding this now, I make a conscious effort to engage in grounding activities whenever I can, knowing how beneficial they are for my overall well-being.

The Cycles of Nature and Personal Growth

Nature's cycles – day and night, the changing seasons, the phases of the moon – are all metaphors for our own lives. These cycles teach us valuable lessons about growth, transformation, and renewal.

By reflecting on how these natural cycles mirror the phases of our own lives, we can find deeper meaning and insight into our personal journeys. Aligning our personal growth with these natural rhythms can bring harmony and balance to our spiritual journeys.

Day and Night: the Daily Cycle of Renewal

The daily cycle of day and night offers a powerful lesson in balance and renewal. Daytime is associated with activity, productivity, and external engagement. It's the time when we're awake, alert and active – much like the Sun that energises and illuminates the world.

In our lives, this can be likened to periods of high energy and productivity when we focus on work, relationships and personal projects.

Nighttime, on the other hand, represents rest, reflection and internal processing. As the world quiets down and the stars emerge, we're reminded of the importance of rest and introspection. This is a time to recharge our bodies and minds, to reflect on the day's events and connect with our inner selves.

By embracing the natural rhythm of day and night, we can ensure a balanced approach to our daily lives, recognising the need for both action and rest.

The Changing Seasons: a Cycle of Growth and Renewal

Each of the four seasons – spring, summer, autumn and winter – carries unique energies and lessons that can guide our personal growth.

Spring is a time of renewal and new beginnings. As the Earth awakens from the dormancy of winter, we see new life sprouting everywhere. Trees bud, flowers bloom and animals come out of hibernation. This season encourages us to embrace new opportunities and start fresh. It's a time to plant seeds, both literally and metaphorically, setting intentions for personal and spiritual growth. Just as the natural world bursts into life, we too can harness this energy to initiate new projects, develop new habits and welcome change into our lives.

Summer represents growth, abundance and the fullness of life. The long, warm days provide ample sunlight for plants to grow and thrive. In our own lives, summer is a time to nurture and develop the seeds we planted in spring. It's a period of active growth, creativity and productivity. Embracing the energy of summer means fully engaging in our pursuits, enjoying the abundance around us and celebrating our progress. It's a time to bask in the warmth of life's joys and to fully participate in the vibrant energy of the season.

Autumn is a season of harvest, reflection and gratitude. As the leaves change colour and fall, and the days grow shorter, we're reminded of the impermanence of life. This is a time to reflect on the growth and accomplishments of the past year, harvest the fruits of our labour and express gratitude for all we have. Autumn encourages us to slow down, to take stock of our lives and to acknowledge both our successes and challenges.

It's a season of balance, where we can appreciate the fullness of life and prepare for the quiet introspection of winter.

Winter is a time of rest, introspection and deep renewal. The cold, dark days prompt us to turn inward, to rest and reflect. Nature itself retreats and hibernates, conserving energy for the renewal of spring. In our own lives, winter offers a valuable opportunity for deep introspection and self-care.

It's a time to rest, to evaluate our lives and to contemplate our personal and spiritual journeys. Embracing the stillness of winter allows us to recharge and prepare for the new beginnings that spring will bring.

The Phases of the Moon: a Cycle of Emotional and Spiritual Growth

The moon's phases – from the new moon to the full moon, and back again – are another powerful symbol of growth and transformation. Each phase of the moon carries unique energies that can guide our emotional and spiritual journeys.

The new moon marks the beginning of the lunar cycle. It's a time of darkness, yet it holds the potential for new beginnings. This phase encourages us to set intentions and envision what we want to bring into our lives.

It's a time to plant the seeds of our desires and to focus on new goals and aspirations. The new moon's energy supports new ventures, personal growth, and spiritual exploration.

As the moon moves from new to full, its waxing phase symbolises growth and development. This is a time to take action on the intentions set during the new moon, to nurture our projects and work towards our goals. The increasing light of the moon reflects our own journey of growth, as we gain clarity, confidence, and momentum. It's a period of building and expanding, supported by the Moon's growing energy.

The full moon is a time of completion, illumination and heightened energy. It represents the peak of the lunar cycle, when the moon is fully illuminated. This phase encourages us to celebrate our achievements, to acknowledge our progress and to gain insight into our lives. The full moon's light can bring clarity to our thoughts and emotions, helping us to see things from a new perspective. It's also a time to release what no longer serves us, making space for new growth.

After the full moon, the waning phase symbolises release and reflection. As the moon's light diminishes, we're encouraged to let go of the things that no longer align with our highest good. This is a time for introspection, for evaluating our lives and making necessary adjustments.

The waning moon supports inner work, healing and preparation for the new cycle ahead. It's a period of winding down, conserving energy and finding balance.

Aligning Personal Growth with Nature's Rhythms

By aligning our personal growth with the cycles of nature, we can cultivate a more harmonious and balanced life. Each cycle, whether daily, seasonal, or lunar, offers unique insights and energies that can support our spiritual journey. Embracing these natural rhythms helps us to stay grounded, flow with life's changes and nurture our personal and spiritual development.

Reflect on how the energy of each cycle resonates with your current life experiences. Use the symbolism of day and night to balance your daily activities and rest.

Embrace the changing seasons to guide your personal growth, recognising when it's time for new beginnings, active growth, reflection or rest. Follow the phases of the Moon to set intentions, take action, celebrate your achievements and release what no longer serves you. By consciously aligning your personal growth with these natural cycles, you can create a more intentional and fulfilling spiritual journey. Nature's rhythms remind us that life is a continuous process of growth, transformation and renewal.

Embracing these cycles allows us to flow with the natural ebb and flow of life, finding balance and harmony along the way. Just as a tree draws strength from its roots and nourishment from the sun, we, too, can find spiritual strength and nourishment through our connection with nature and everything around us to achieve a deeper sense of peace, balance and harmony in our lives.

Nature invites us to slow down, breathe deeply and remember our innate connection to the Earth and all living beings. Allow the Earth's comforting presence to guide you on your spiritual path.

How to Ground Yourself

There are so many ways that we can reconnect and ground ourselves with the energy of the Earth. Find what works best for you – I'll list my personal favourites below:

Walk barefoot outdoors. Spend at least 30 minutes per day walking barefoot on natural surfaces like grass, sand, soil or even concrete. I try to do this mostly in the summer, because who wants to be walking around getting frostbite in the depths of winter? If I'm at my local park, walking my dog, I'll often take off my shoes and socks on the grass and walk barefoot. Similarly, whenever we go to the beach, my footwear is off on the promenade, before I even get near the beach itself.

This simple practice helps me feel more grounded, reduces my stress levels and gives me a sense of freedom and connection with nature. The texture of the Earth beneath my feet and the coolness of the grass provide a soothing and invigorating experience that refreshes my mind and body. Walking barefoot has become one of my favourite ways to quickly and effectively reconnect with the natural world.

Use grounding products. There are so many products out there these days such as grounding mats, sheets and bands that are all designed to simulate the effects of walking barefoot by connecting you to the Earth's energy indoors. Personally, I have a grounding sheet on our bed which plugs into the wall (an earthed socket), so that each night I can let my body naturally recharge itself whilst I sleep. We spend a third of our lives in bed – let that sink in! This requires no extra time and allows all of that static energy to be released from my body whilst I have a restful night's sleep.

I've noticed a significant improvement in the quality of my sleep and a reduction in the muscle tension and stress that I often feel at the end of the day. These grounding products make it easy to incorporate the benefits of grounding into a busy lifestyle, ensuring that I stay connected to the Earth's energy even when I can't spend as much time outdoors as I'd like.

Gardening. Any activity that involves direct contact with soil can also provide grounding benefits. Whether you're cutting the grass or potting up plants, gardening can help you reconnect with that natural energy. The simple act of digging your hands into the soil, planting seeds and nurturing growth allows you to absorb the Earth's energy directly.

Gardening also provides a sense of accomplishment and connection to the cycles of nature, which can be incredibly therapeutic. It's a meditative activity that encourages mindfulness and presence, allowing you to tune into the rhythms of the natural world. Through cultivating plants, you cultivate a deeper sense of grounding, peace and well-being.

Swimming in natural water bodies. Swimming in the likes of lakes, rivers or the ocean can also ground you, as water is a good conductor of electricity. Cold-water swimming has become increasingly popular as of late with those wanting to feel a connection with the Earth. I did it myself a couple of times back in 2022, and although I hated it at the time, the "buzz" and feeling of adrenaline that shot around my body for hours afterwards was undeniable. It was as if the cold water had reset my system, leaving me feeling invigorated and deeply alive.

This experience not only grounded me physically but also mentally, providing a clear mind and a renewed sense of energy and vitality. The combination of cold-water immersion and grounding made me appreciate the impact that nature can have on our overall well-being, encouraging me to incorporate these practices more regularly into my life. Admittedly, I've only been cold-water swimming once since, but it's definitely something that I would do again should I find the right tribe to do it with.

Using crystals. Each type of crystal has unique properties that can aid in balancing and stabilising your energy. As we spoke about in Chapter 7, crystals are natural conductors of the Earth's energy and so can be powerful tools for grounding. Stones like hematite, black tourmaline, and smoky quartz are particularly effective. I carry a piece of hematite with me most days and often meditate with it in my hand. The weight and coolness of the crystal help me feel centred and connected to the Earth's grounding energy.

Placing crystals around your living space or wearing them as jewellery can also help maintain a grounded state throughout the day. Integrating crystals into your daily routine requires minimal effort but can significantly enhance your connection to the natural world and promote that sense of balance and calm.

Meditation. To start, find a quiet spot, preferably in a natural setting like a park or garden. Once there, remove your shoes to allow your feet to make direct contact with the Earth. Close your eyes and take a few deep breaths, inhaling slowly through your nose and exhaling through your mouth. As you breathe, visualise roots extending from the soles of your feet deep into the Earth, anchoring you firmly to the ground. Imagine the Earth's energy flowing up through these roots into your body, filling you with a sense of calm and stability.

Focus on the sensations in your body, the sounds of nature around you and your breath, maintaining this meditative state for at least ten minutes. Afterward, take a moment to reflect on how you feel, noting any thoughts or insights that arise.

Nature-based mindfulness walk. Choose a natural setting, such as a forest trail, a beach, or a park. As you begin your walk, slow down and pay close attention to your surroundings. Notice the colours and shapes of the leaves, the texture of the ground beneath your feet and the sounds of birds or rustling leaves.

Breathe deeply and evenly, using each breath to anchor yourself in the present moment. If your mind starts to wander, gently bring your focus back to your immediate environment. This exercise not only grounds you but also enhances your appreciation for the natural world, fostering a deeper sense of connection and tranquillity.

Forest bathing. The Japanese practice of Shinrin-yoku, or "forest bathing," involves immersing ourselves in a forest environment to enhance health and well-being. Studies have shown that even short periods spent in nature can significantly reduce cortisol levels, the hormone associated with stress, leading to a more relaxed and balanced state of mind[15].

The word "forest" can literally be broken down into "for rest," highlighting the natural environment's inherent ability to provide relaxation and respite. As you walk through the forest, the sights, sounds and scents of the trees and plants create a sensory experience that calms the mind and body. The act of being present in such a tranquil setting allows you to disconnect from daily stressors and reconnect with your inner self, promoting a sense of peace and rejuvenation. When we integrate grounding practices into our daily routines, we can harness the Earth's natural energy to support our physical and mental well-being, fostering a deeper connection with nature and enhancing our overall health.

Activity

Take a leisurely walk in a natural setting, focusing on the sights, sounds and smells around you. Practice mindfulness by being fully present in the moment, and appreciating the beauty and serenity of your surroundings.

Embrace a tree and feel its solid, stable presence.

This act can help you feel more grounded and connected to the natural world. Trees have long been symbols of strength and stability, and their energy can be incredibly grounding.

How did you feel before and after your grounding meditation?

What changes did you notice in your body and mind?

How can you incorporate more nature-based practices into your daily routine?

In what ways do you feel a stronger connection to the Earth and all living beings?

Chapter 13
Sacred Rituals

Think about rituals as the secret sauce that spices up your daily routine, except they're everywhere. Whether it's how you make your bed in the morning, the way you brew your perfect cup of tea or even the little dance you do when your favourite song comes on the radio – these are all rituals. They're the familiar moves in a dance we all perform, helping us groove through our days with a spring in our step.

But why should we care about these daily dances?

More than just keeping us on the beat, rituals ground us, giving each day a bit of structure and a whole lot of meaning. Imagine starting your day without your usual cuppa, or skipping that bedtime story with your kids – feels off, right?

That's the power of rituals at work.

From the tiny personal habits to the big, festive family gatherings, rituals connect us to our history and to each other. They're the golden threads tying us to generations past and future. These aren't just fancy traditions; they're ways for people to find their spot in the community and the Universe.

Let's not forget how good rituals are for our brains. Sticking to a ritual can turn a stressful day into a manageable one. It's like having a magic wand that can make worries shrink and confidence grow. When we share these rituals with others, at weddings or celebrations, it's like we're all joining in on a group hug. It makes us feel part of something bigger, giving us a sense of belonging and support.

As we go through this chapter, think about the rituals in your life as more than just habits. They're your personal and communal superpowers, turning ordinary moments into magical ones. Ready to explore how these everyday enchantments work and how you can sprinkle more of them into your life?

Rituals and ceremonies are structured actions performed in a particular sequence, often for a specific purpose. While both terms are sometimes used interchangeably, they do have subtle differences.

A ritual usually refers to a set of actions or activities performed regularly, often with a symbolic meaning or intent, such as meditation each morning, or lighting a candle to honour someone's memory.

A ceremony, however, is a formal or structured event, often marking a significant occasion or transition, such as weddings, graduations, or spiritual gatherings. Ceremonies typically involve a series of intentional actions, symbols or traditions that hold deep meaning, like exchanging vows, offering blessings, or performing rites of passage to honour life's important moments or milestones.

Throughout history, both rituals and ceremonies have played vital roles in every civilisation across the globe. They're the threads that weave together the fabric of social and cultural identity. For example, ancient Egyptians performed elaborate rituals for the dead, believing they ensured safe passage and a peaceful afterlife, and Native American tribes have held ceremonies to celebrate the seasonal cycles of nature, each filled with rituals that honour their deep connection to the Earth.

In many cultures, rituals and ceremonies are ways to mark important life events, celebrate victories, mourn losses, and transmit cherished values from one generation to the next.

Psychological Impact of Rituals

Participating in or creating rituals and ceremonies can have a huge psychological impact on us. They provide structure and meaning in life, helping us to process emotions and navigate life's changes. For instance, a simple ritual like lighting a candle on the anniversary of a loved one's passing can offer solace and a moment of reflection.

Scientific studies show that engaging in rituals can reduce anxiety, improve performance and increase confidence[16]. This is because rituals often create a sense of control and order, making unpredictable events seem more manageable.

Rituals can also strengthen community bonds. When we participate in ceremonies together, like a graduation or a religious festival, it fosters a sense of belonging and shared identity. This communal aspect can be incredibly supportive, providing a network of social and emotional support.

So when we think about it, rituals and ceremonies aren't just about tradition; they're active, powerful practices that shape how we understand the world, connect with others, and find our place in the Universe. They remind us of our history, connect us with our present, and give us hope for the future.

Why Rituals Matter Personally

As we learn about the significance of rituals, consider how they're not just cultural artefacts but personal necessities. Integrating rituals is about constructing a framework that supports your emotional and psychological well-being.

Imagine for a moment the consequences of a life devoid of these anchoring practices: Days may become shapeless, leaving you more susceptible to stress and disconnected from your own emotions and those of the people around you.

On the flip side, embracing ritualistic practices can elevate your quality of life significantly. It can transform how you approach each day, infuse your life with joy and purpose and help you navigate challenges with resilience. Engaging regularly in rituals tailored to your needs can enhance your mood, sharpen your focus and deepen your connection with others.

The Transformative Power of Rituals

As we explore the different types of rituals and how to create your own, consider how integrating these practices into your daily life can not only preserve cherished traditions but also impact your personal development. Rituals and ceremonies are powerful tools that shape how we understand the world, connect with others and find our place in the Universe. They remind us of our history, connect us with our present and inspire our future.

At this point, I'd like you to remember that the power of these practices lies in their ability to transform ordinary moments into something sacred.

The Intention Behind the Practice

Back in 2022, I was driving myself home from work whilst listening away to a random podcast, where the hosts were trying to debunk the Law of Attraction and why they thought that it works for some, and not for others. The conversation went into real depth about whether or not crystals were just a placebo effect, and if visualisation only works because it's tricking your mind. And in that moment, it made me think: It's not what you do; it's how you do it.

This really struck a chord with me, because it made me start thinking about everything I do, and why it works for me. You may have heard the phrase, "It's not the size of the boat, it's the motion of the ocean" before.

It's so true!

For example, let's take a little ritual that I do on the first of each month. This is quite an old-style witchy thing to do, but on the morning of the 1st of each month, I grab some cinnamon and head to my front door. I stand on my porch, looking inward, and pop some cinnamon into my hand. I then clasp my fingers around it and hold my hand to my heart centre, before closing my eyes and physically speaking into existence what I want in terms of abundance and wealth.

"OK, cinnamon, as I hold you in my hand, I ask you to channel wealth and abundance into my life. Attract financial blessings and open the doors to new opportunities for me. May my path be cleared for success and wealth to flow freely towards me. Thank you for your vibrant energy," I'll say, and then I'll open my eyes and blow the handful of cinnamon across the threshold of my house, almost visualising it as money blowing into my home.

Cinnamon has been cherished for centuries, not just for its rich flavour, but also for its reputed magical properties, particularly in attracting wealth. Ancient civilisations believed that the warm, sweet aroma of cinnamon could draw prosperity and success, making it a staple in many rituals and spells. Even today, many sprinkle cinnamon in their wallets or use cinnamon-scented candles to set intentions for financial growth and manifest greater abundance in their lives.

My neighbours must watch me doing this on the first of each month and think I'm some sort of crazy person, but honestly, it works wonders for me! I put a video of myself doing this on TikTok back in 2022 and the amount of comments I got in response was insane.

"How is that doing anything?", or "How does that even work and deliver you money?" they asked.

Well, it's all in the intention: It isn't what you do, it's the way that you do it.

When I pour that cinnamon onto my hand and close my eyes, I stand for about two minutes, visualising money in my bank account.

I visualise buying myself upgraded things, I visualise myself happy and wealthy. I visualise myself as abundant and prosperous. Almost to the point that when I open my eyes to blow the cinnamon, I startle myself with where I am, because I've been living that visualisation as real life for those last two minutes.

And that's why I find that rituals like that work for me – because I've put intention behind it.

I knew what I wanted.

I created a little ritual.

I felt the energy of what I wanted and connected to it.

I took that little action of blowing the cinnamon.

For some people, a ritual like that wouldn't work, but I dare to bet that, for those that it didn't work, they might have simply tipped the cinnamon into their hands and blown, without giving any prior attention or instruction. So there's no meaning behind what they've just done – as though they've just done it on autopilot and they don't care about the outcome.

Intention acts as the driving force behind our thoughts, feelings, and actions.

It's the underlying motivation that directs our energy towards a particular outcome. When it comes to the Law of Attraction, the intention behind our actions is everything. It's the guiding principle that determines the quality of our manifestations and shapes the overall experience.

Intention helps us align with the natural flow of the Universe. When our intentions are rooted in positivity, authenticity and a desire for the highest good, we resonate with the universal energy. That alignment creates a fertile ground for the manifestation of our desires, as the Universe responds favourably to intentions driven by love and harmony.

Intention acts as a catalyst for personal growth and transformation. By setting clear intentions, we challenge and overcome limiting beliefs that may hinder our progress. Intention empowers us to step out of our comfort zones, break free from self-imposed limitations and expand our realm of possibilities.

Intention also instils within us a sense of purpose and resilience. When setbacks arise, a strong intention keeps us motivated and focused on our goals. It provides the strength to persist in the face of challenges, learn from failures and adapt our approach as needed. It fuels our determination to keep moving forward, ultimately leading us to our desired outcomes.

In the pursuit of achieving our goals and aspirations, the importance of intention is paramount. Yes, actions can play a significant role in bringing about desired outcomes, but it's the infusion of intention that amplifies their impact. By understanding and harnessing the power of intention, we can optimise our efforts, navigate challenges with clarity, and ultimately get the best results.

The intention is the driving force behind our actions. It gives them purpose and meaning. It's the conscious decision to align our thoughts, beliefs and desires with our chosen course of action. By infusing intention into our actions, we elevate them from just simple mechanical movements to intentional steps towards our desired manifestations.

The more energy we dedicate to something, the greater the potential for a positive result.

For example, you'll more than likely have a personal goal or aspiration in mind that you want to achieve in the next six months. If you approach it with a half-hearted effort, your results are likely to reflect that level of commitment and you'll be met with half-arsed results. But, when we wholeheartedly invest our energy, focus and passion into achieving our goals, we set in motion a chain of events that aligns with our intentions and increases the likelihood of success.

This idea also holds true in interpersonal relationships. The energy we bring into our interactions shapes the quality of our connections with others. When we approach others with kindness, empathy and positivity, we create an atmosphere of warmth and understanding. This, in turn, fosters trust, deepens relationships and enhances the overall outcome of our interactions.

It's important to note that the principle of investing energy doesn't secure a guarantee of immediate success or that positive thinking alone can solve all problems. Instead, it highlights the power of intentionality and the role of focused energy in shaping our experiences. It encourages us to align our actions, thoughts and emotions towards our desired outcomes, amplifying our efforts and increasing the probability of favourable results.

I really hope that this chapter helps to inspire you when you're going about your daily routines, your rituals, your crystal healing, or whatever it is that you're doing... just remember to make sure that you do it with intention!

Rituals aren't just mere routines. They're intentional acts that infuse our days with meaning and offer a conduit to connect deeply with our inner selves and the world around us. Each ritual, whether it marks the beginning of a day or an important life transition, is a reaffirmation of our values and our intentions. They allow us to pause, reflect and align our actions with our deepest desires and beliefs.

Imagine a life where each day begins with purpose and each significant moment is acknowledged and celebrated.

What could this do for our sense of presence and fulfilment?

Rituals offer us a toolkit to craft a life that feels more connected and intentional. By embedding these sacred practices into the fabric of our everyday existence, we not only honour our personal journey but also elevate our capacity to engage with life in a more meaningful way. Let us then move forward with the wisdom that rituals aren't just acts we perform, but are, in fact, a way to sculpt our lives, moulding our days into shapes that resonate with our soul's deepest desires.

Lunar Rituals

The lunar cycle, marking the moon's journey around the Earth, holds deep spiritual significance in many cultures. Each phase of the moon symbolises a different aspect of life, growth, and renewal.

The new moon represents beginnings and new opportunities, making it an ideal time to set intentions and start new projects.

Conversely, the full moon is a period of culmination and fruition, perfect for reflection, releasing what no longer serves you and manifesting the intentions set during the new moon.

Conducting New Moon Rituals

New moon rituals focus on setting intentions for what you wish to grow in the coming lunar month. Here's a simple guide to conducting your own new moon ritual:

Prepare your space. Choose a quiet, comfortable spot where you won't be disturbed. You might like to clean the area physically or smudge it with sage to clear old energies.

Gather your tools. Typical items might include candles, paper and pen, crystals, and any personal items that symbolise new beginnings for you.

Meditate and reflect. Spend a few minutes in meditation, focusing on your breath and clearing your mind. Reflect on what you wish to attract or achieve in the coming month.

Set your intentions. Write your intentions on paper. Be clear and precise. It helps to phrase these positively, focusing on what you want to draw into your life.

Visualise and affirm. Close your eyes and visualise your intentions coming to fruition. Speak your intentions aloud to affirm them to the universe.

Close the ritual. Thank the Universe or any higher power you believe in for their guidance. Snuff out the candle and keep your written intentions in a safe place where you can revisit them.

Conducting Full Moon Rituals

Full moon rituals are about release and manifestation, perfect for letting go of what no longer serves you and reinforcing what you're bringing into your life. Here's how to conduct a full moon ritual:

Prepare your space. Ensure your space is clean and quiet like with the new moon ritual. You may want to use sage, palo santo, or even incense to purify the area.

Gather your tools. Arrange candles, a bowl of water (to represent the full moon), your crystals, and any notes you have from the new moon ritual regarding what you hoped to manifest.

Release what no longer serves. Reflect on the past month and identify anything that's holding you back. Write these down on paper. I often choose to burn the paper as a symbolic release at the end of my ritual.

Reaffirm your intentions. Revisit the intentions set during the new moon. Spend a moment visualising these goals as realised realities. Feel the emotions that come with achieving these dreams.

Close the ritual. Give thanks to the Universe or your higher power. Feel gratitude for the growth and learning that's come with this lunar cycle. Save or release your notes as you see fit, and snuff out the candles.

Engaging regularly with the lunar cycles through these rituals can deeply enhance your personal growth and manifestation abilities. By aligning your spiritual practices with the natural rhythms of the moon, you not only harmonise your inner energy but also tap into a greater cosmic flow, enhancing your ability to manifest your desires and release what hinders your progress.

Seasonal Rituals

The changing of seasons is an incredible and enduring cycle that affects not only the environment around us, but also influences our internal landscape. Seasonal transitions – marked by the equinoxes and solstices – are celebrated across various cultures and spiritual traditions for their deep symbolic meanings.

The equinoxes, occurring in the spring and autumn, symbolise balance and equality between day and night.

In contrast, the solstices, occurring in summer and winter, represent the peak and nadir of the sun's journey through the sky, highlighting themes of peak vitality and deep rest, respectively.

Each season brings its own unique energy and focusing on these can help to harness the particular qualities each one offers:

Spring equinox ritual. Around March 20th or 21st. This marks the beginning of Spring in the Northern Hemisphere when the day and night are approximately equal in length. Celebrate new beginnings and renewal by planting new seeds literally and metaphorically. Start by cleaning your living space thoroughly, then plant new seeds in your garden or in pots. As you do, set intentions for what you wish to grow in your life. Incorporate green candles and fresh flowers to symbolise new life and growth.

Summer solstice ritual. Around June 20th or 21st. This is the longest day of the year in the Northern Hemisphere, signalling the start of Summer. Embrace the fullness of life and the energy of abundance. Create a ritual around the fire element, which could involve lighting a bonfire or candles. Write down what you've achieved so far and your gratitude for these accomplishments. This is also a time to celebrate the strength and passion within you, perhaps with vibrant music and dance.

Autumn equinox ritual. Around September 22nd or 23rd. Similar to the spring equinox, this equinox marks the start of autumn in the Northern Hemisphere with day and night being approximately equal. Reflect on balance and harvest. As this is a time for reaping what has been sown, gather friends for a meal where everyone brings a dish, ideally made from seasonal produce. Create a gratitude tree by writing what you are thankful for on leaves or pieces of paper and attaching them to branches placed in a vase.

Winter solstice ritual. Around December 21st or 22nd. This day has the shortest period of daylight and the longest night in the Northern Hemisphere, marking the beginning of winter. Honour introspection and rebirth. This is the perfect time for a quiet, reflective ritual. Light candles and spend time meditating on what you wish to let go of and what you hope to rebirth in the coming year. Consider writing these reflections in a journal and setting intentions that focus on inner peace and renewal.

Aligning with the natural cycles through these seasonal rituals can truly enhance your personal well-being and spiritual connection. These rituals allow us to tap into the rhythmic flow of nature, reminding us that we're part of a larger, interconnected cosmos.

By observing the unique qualities of each season, we can mirror these changes internally – growing when the world grows, harvesting our accomplishments as the world slows, letting go during times of decline and conserving our energy when renewal is necessary.

These practices not only foster a deep connection with the natural world but also help us to adjust our lives according to the natural laws of change and growth.

Engaging in seasonal rituals provides us with opportunities to pause and reflect, make necessary changes and move forward with greater harmony and awareness. This conscious participation in the cycles of nature can bring about a more balanced lifestyle, enhanced health and a deeper sense of peace.

Daily Rituals for Connection and Mindfulness

Incorporating daily rituals into your routine can be a transformative way to enhance overall well-being, foster mindfulness and cultivate a deeper connection with yourself. Here are some effective ways to develop simple yet powerful daily rituals:

Morning meditation. Start your day centred and calm by dedicating a few minutes each morning to meditation. This can be as simple as sitting in a quiet place and focusing on your breath, using guided meditations or practising mindfulness meditation to observe your thoughts without judgement.

Gratitude practice. Each morning or evening, take a moment to reflect on and write down three things you are grateful for. This practice can shift your mindset from one of lack to one of abundance, helping to enhance your mood and perspective throughout the day.

Evening journaling. Wind down at the end of the day with a journaling session. Reflect on the day's events, jot down what you learned and express any emotions you experienced. This can serve as a therapeutic way to clear your mind and facilitate better sleep.

The implementation of daily rituals can greatly impact your mental and emotional health by providing stability and structure. Regular rituals add a comforting rhythm to daily life, promoting a sense of security and predictability that can ease anxiety and stress. Engaging in consistent daily practices helps cultivate a state of mindfulness, keeping you fully present in your activities and reducing the mental clutter that can distract you from living in the moment. Regular self-care and mindfulness practices contribute to overall emotional health, reducing symptoms of depression and anxiety and increasing feelings of happiness and contentment.

These simple, daily rituals can transform your day-to-day life. By dedicating time to these practices, you reinforce your commitment to self-care and mindfulness, paving the way for a more centred, peaceful and fulfilling life.

Rituals for Healing and Release

Rituals can play a critical role in healing emotional wounds and releasing past traumas. These practices often incorporate symbolic elements that facilitate letting go, transformation and new beginnings:

Water rituals for cleansing. Utilise the purifying properties of water to help wash away negative energies and emotions. Ritual baths, enhanced with Epsom salts, essential oils and herbs, can provide physical and spiritual cleansing, aiding in emotional detox.

Fire rituals for release. Fire can serve as a powerful tool for transformation and release. Writing down the things you wish to let go of on a piece of paper and safely burning it can be a potent act of release, helping to clear out old patterns and pain.

Using incantations and affirmations. Reciting specific affirmations or mantras during rituals can reinforce the intentions of healing and release. Phrases should be chosen to support letting go of the past and embracing healing, such as "I release what no longer serves me" or "I embrace healing and renewal."

By regularly engaging in these rituals, you can create a sacred space for healing and transformation, allowing you to move forward with greater clarity and peace. Whether you're seeking to heal emotional scars or release burdensome memories, these practices offer a pathway to deeper self-awareness and renewed strength.

Creating Your Own Rituals

Creating personal rituals that resonate with your beliefs and spiritual needs can be an empowering way to enhance your spiritual practice. You could incorporate objects, symbols or elements that hold personal or spiritual significance. This could be anything from a family heirloom to natural elements like stones or water, which represent personal or universal meanings.

When it comes to choosing a dedicated area in your home where you can perform your rituals, this space should be a reflection of what feels sacred to you and can be adorned with items that elevate your spiritual practice, such as icons, texts, or natural elements.

Whether it's lighting a candle, writing down intentions or reciting a prayer or affirmation, intentional actions that are repeated in a ritualistic manner can help manifest spiritual intentions and foster a deeper connection to the divine.

Utilise incense, sound, tactile objects and visual elements to engage all senses and enhance the spiritual experience. This multisensory approach can deepen the emotional and spiritual impact of the ritual.

Above all else, allow your rituals to evolve as your spiritual needs change. Flexibility ensures that your practices remain relevant and meaningful, facilitating an ongoing and deepening relationship with the divine.

Crafting your own rituals is a deeply personal process that allows you to connect with your beliefs, intentions and the rhythms of your daily life in a meaningful way. To design rituals that resonate with you, there are a few key elements to consider:

Timing. Choose when to perform your ritual based on its purpose. Morning rituals can set a positive tone for the day, while evening rituals might help in unwinding and reflecting. Align your ritual with natural cycles like the lunar phases or seasons if they hold significance for you.

Components. Decide what physical elements you want to include in your ritual. These could be candles, incense, water, or crystals – each bringing its own energy and significance. Also, consider whether you want your ritual to include movement, such as yoga or walking, or be more still and meditative.

Setting. The environment where you conduct your ritual should reflect its purpose and enhance its meaning. This could be a designated quiet corner of your home, a garden or anywhere that you find peaceful and conducive to introspection and focus.

Symbols. Incorporate symbols that have personal or universal meanings. These could be anything from religious icons to personal mementos that symbolise your intentions or desires.

Creativity and personalisation. Let your imagination guide you. Your ritual should be a reflection of who you are. Feel free to adapt traditional practices or invent entirely new ones that better suit your lifestyle and spiritual beliefs.

By thoughtfully combining these elements, you can create a ritual that not only aligns with your personal and spiritual needs but also has the flexibility to evolve as you do.

Rituals have the transformative power to not just mark the significant moments of our lives but also to enhance our daily experiences, providing a structured way to deepen our connections with ourselves and the world around us. By integrating rituals into your routine, you can create moments of pause, reflection and connection in an otherwise hectic life.

These practices encourage continuous exploration and adaptation, allowing them to grow and change as you do. As your needs and circumstances evolve, so too can your rituals. This adaptability ensures that they remain meaningful and supportive over time, providing a steady source of strength and comfort.

Whilst creativity and personalisation are encouraged, maintaining the sanctity and integrity of your rituals is crucial. They should be treated with respect and thoughtfulness, ensuring that they remain a positive and grounding force in your life.

As you continue to explore and integrate these practices, you'll likely find that they bring not only structure and stability, but also a sense of fulfilment and peace.

Activity

I want you to craft a ritual that aligns with your personal and spiritual goals.

Set your intention. Decide what you want to achieve with your ritual. Write down one clear intention.

Gather elements. Choose items that resonate with your intention, such as candles for focus, crystals for energy, or essential oils for atmosphere.

Choose a time and place. Pick a consistent time and a quiet place where you can perform your ritual undisturbed.

Outline the ritual. Plan the steps of your ritual. Start by lighting a candle, then spend a few minutes in meditation or affirmation, and conclude by jotting down any insights or expressing gratitude.

Practise regularly. Incorporate your ritual into your daily or weekly routine to deepen its impact and your connection to its purpose.

Reflect and adapt. Periodically review the effectiveness of your ritual and make adjustments to reflect your evolving needs.

This streamlined approach allows you to easily integrate a meaningful ritual into your life, enhancing your spiritual practice and personal growth.

Chapter 14
Bringing It All Together

B efore opening my mind to any of these spiritual and well-being techniques, I would constantly feel anxious, on edge and lacking in confidence.

My life always felt like it was meant to have a purpose, but I just couldn't see the wood for the trees.

Once I began to embrace these practices, something shifted within me. The fog of doubt and fear started to lift, revealing a path that had always been there, waiting for me to walk it. Each step I took was guided by a newfound sense of clarity and inner peace.

I discovered that the power to transform my life had always been within me, and by nurturing my spirit, I unlocked a reservoir of strength and resilience. Now, I move forward with confidence. I know now that my life is filled with purpose, and that I'm equipped to navigate any challenge that comes my way.

The journey is ongoing, but with each day, I grow closer to the person I was always meant to be.

My reason for writing this book was for it to be far more than a simple guide – I wanted it to be a gateway that helps you open up to the immense possibilities that life has to offer. The practices and insights contained within these pages are potent tools, carefully crafted to help you lay down a solid foundation of awareness and self-harmony.

They're designed to support your journey towards a life brimming with fulfilment and contentment, transforming the way you view and interact with the world around you.

Each chapter and each exercise has been structured not just to inform, but to inspire, to ignite a spark of change that can grow into a consuming fire of transformation. As you integrate these practices into your life, you'll find that even the most mundane activities can be transformed into rich opportunities for personal growth and deep happiness.

The knowledge and strategies you've acquired are not merely for temporary application, but for a lifelong commitment to exploring the greater potentials of existence.

Imagine this not as the conclusion of the book, but as the beginning of an extraordinary adventure. This will be a continuous process of discovery, learning and profound realisation.

I also hope that by now, you've realised that there is so much more to this life than previously imagined. There are depths yet to be discovered, heights yet to be soared and horizons that stretch infinitely. With each day, with every use of the tools and insights from this book, you're invited to push further, to explore more deeply and to live more fully.

Step into this journey with confidence and curiosity. Let each decision be guided by a newfound understanding and a refreshed perspective. Embrace the challenges and opportunities with open arms, ready to transform them into stepping stones towards your ultimate aspirations.

Reflecting on Integration

As you integrate these spiritual practices into your daily life, take time to reflect on their impact.

Which practices bring you the most peace? Which ones help you feel more connected to yourself and the world around you? Could these moments of reflection help you appreciate the journey of integration more deeply?

As you integrate these new spiritual practices, use these guiding questions to deepen your commitment and understanding:

How can these small moments of mindfulness transform the overall quality of my day?

In what ways can I tailor these practices to better suit my personal and spiritual growth?

What barriers do I need to overcome to make these practices a consistent part of my life?

How does each practice serve my broader life goals and values?

By reflecting on these questions and actively seeking to integrate mindfulness into every part of your day, you turn what might once have been fleeting moments into transformative opportunities for growth and reflection. This isn't just about adding to your life, it's about enriching the life you already live.

The true essence of this book is to prove that spirituality and personal well-being don't exist in a vacuum separate from your daily life. Rather, spirituality is woven through every moment and every breath. As you begin to view these practices as quality enhancements to your daily life rather than tasks to check off, you'll find that incorporating them into your routine becomes easier and more natural.

The journey of personal and spiritual growth is an ever-evolving one, mirroring the constant changes and developments in our lives. Just as the seasons cycle through phases of growth, harvest and renewal, so too must our spiritual practices adapt and evolve to stay aligned with our shifting needs and circumstances.

As we go through life, we encounter a variety of experiences that shape and redefine us. Our understanding deepens, our experiences broaden and inevitably, our spiritual needs and responses evolve.

It's essential to acknowledge that what serves us at one point may not be as effective under different conditions or stages of life. Recognising this is the first step in cultivating a flexible and responsive approach to our spiritual practices.

To make sure that our spiritual practices continue to serve our highest good, it's important to engage in regular reflection and self-assessment. This can be a formal process, such as a monthly or yearly review, where you take time to reflect on each practice's effectiveness and personal relevance.

In these sessions, you can ask yourself:

How have my spiritual practices enhanced my daily life?

Do these activities still resonate with my current spiritual needs?

What emotions or thoughts arise as I engage in these practices?

These reflective questions will serve as a guide to gauge the current alignment of your spiritual activities with your personal growth.

For further spiritual self-development, you can visit cannycrystalsacademy.co.uk, where you'll discover courses, workshops and other resources to empower you on the journey ahead.

You can also listen to the Canny Crystals podcast, available for free across all streaming platforms, with a new episode out every Friday. Just type "Canny Crystals" on the search bar!

A Final Thought

As I dot the final i's and cross the last t's of this book, I can't help but laugh at the serendipitous timing. What started in our comfy, somewhat cramped living room with my fiancé Jonny, our ever-enthusiastic pup JJ and a boatload of dreams, has blossomed into something beautifully bigger.

When I first started scribbling down my thoughts for this book, I was eager to sprinkle a bit of wisdom here and connect some dots there – not just for you, my fantastic readers, but to add a splash of magic to my own life too!

But, oh, what a twist the plot took!

As the chapters of this book filled up, so did our family photo album.

Enter stage left: our baby boy, born January 2024, an addition we joyously welcomed through adoption. This little tyke has turned our world topsy-turvy, painting our lives with a vibrancy and sweetness that's better felt than described.

Every lesson this book holds, every spiritual nugget I've shared, has been tested and proven in the riot of giggles, sleep deprivation, bedtime snuggles and wide-eyed wonder of a baby discovering the world for the very first time.

This adoption journey hasn't just filled our home with laughter, it's etched deeper meaning into every page I've written. The spiritual practices and heart-to-hearts we've explored? They're no longer just theories but are alive and kicking in the warm and busy corners of our home.

As our family has grown in unexpected, wonderful ways throughout the writing of this book, I hope your world broadens to include new forms of love, bursts of joy and serendipitous blessings.

Here's to living with intention and mindfulness, and to appreciating the beauty of each moment. Let each step be a conscious move towards crafting your ideal existence, cherishing the journey as much as the destination.

Embrace this journey with heart and hope, and may every step you take towards fulfilling your dreams remind you that the possibilities within you truly are limitless.

About the Author

Mart Tweedy is a 37-year-old dedicated dad who knows firsthand the depths of struggle and the heights of transformation. His story is one of resilience, self-discovery and the power of believing in our true potential.

Back in 2019, Mart faced what he describes as the darkest period of his life. His beloved granda, a figure of strength and wisdom in his life, passed away suddenly, leaving Mart engulfed in a wave of grief that seemed insurmountable. At the time, Mart was working in the mental health sector of the National Health Service (NHS), helping others navigate their emotional turmoil. Yet, the cruel irony was that he couldn't find a way out of his own grief and depression. The weight of his loss pressed down on him, and despite his knowledge and experience in mental health, he felt trapped in a seemingly endless cycle of sorrow.

One evening, Mart reached a breaking point. In a moment that he now describes as a brief flash of insanity – or perhaps divine clarity – he called out for help to whoever or whatever might be listening. That desperate plea marked the beginning of a profound spiritual journey that would change his life forever. Mart began to explore new paths of healing, discovering the power of crystal healing, mindfulness, gratitude and visualisation techniques. These practices became his lifeline, tools that helped him slowly but surely climb out of the deep, dark pit he believed he was stuck in.

With a renewed sense of purpose and a growing belief in the transformative power of spirituality, Mart decided to share his journey and what he had learned with others. In 2021, with only £250 left in his bank account and a heart full of hope, he launched his own website, cannycrystals.co.uk. Initially, he saw it as a small venture that might bring in a little extra pocket money each month. However, as he put himself out there and confronted his fears head-on, something remarkable happened. By believing in his own worth and the value of his experiences, Mart unlocked a drive and determination within himself that he never knew existed.

In just one year, his business took off beyond his wildest dreams. What started as a modest website quickly blossomed into a thriving enterprise. Mart was soon generating more in one month than he had earned in an entire year working for the NHS. This incredible success gave him the confidence to take the leap into full-time self-employment, leaving behind the security of his NHS job to fully commit to his passion.

Over the next three years, Mart's business would go on to generate nearly £750,000 in revenue – a figure that still amazes him. But perhaps even more rewarding than the financial success was the impact he was making. He was even able to retire his mam, who now proudly works alongside him, helping out wherever possible.

Mart's journey didn't stop there. His podcast quickly climbed the charts, becoming the #1 podcast in the UK for Spirituality week after week. His voice, filled with authenticity and experience, resonated with thousands. Over 30,000 people have enrolled in his online academy, which is centred around spiritual well-being and self-development. Through his teachings, Mart has empowered people from all walks of life to find hope, healing and purpose.

He's since gone on to work with the likes of *British Vogue*, Chanel, Stella McCartney and more recently, Fearne Cotton's Happy Place Festival.

Today, Mart is a beacon of inspiration for anyone facing their own struggles. He understands the depths of despair but also knows the incredible heights we can reach when we confront our fears, embrace our true worth and take bold steps toward a better future. His mission now is to help others find the light within themselves, to break free from whatever holds them back and to discover the true meaning and potential of their lives.

His story is a testament to the fact that, no matter how dark things may seem, there is always a path to transformation and a way to turn pain into purpose.

References

[1] B. Robinson, 'The 90-Second Rule That Builds Self-Control', *Psychology Today*, 2020, https://www.psychologytoday.com/us/blog/the-right-mindset/202004/the-90-second-rule-builds-self-control, (accessed 14 October 2024).

[2] K. Lawson, 'How Do Thoughts and Emotions Affect Health?', Minneapolis, *University of Minnesota*, 2020, https://www.takingcharge.csh.umn.edu/how-do-thoughts-and-emotions-affect-health, (accessed 14 October 2024).

[3] D. Orenstein, 'Small Studies of 40-Hertz Sensory Stimulation Confirm Safety, Suggest Alzheimer's Benefits', Cambridge, *Massachusetts Institute of Technology*, 2022, https://news.mit.edu/2022/small-studies-40hz-sensory-stimulation-confirm-safety-suggest-alzheimers-benefits-1213, (accessed 14 October 2024).

[4] J. Donovan, 'Healing the Body with Frequencies: The Basics Explained', *Sound Health*, 2023, https://www.donovanhealth.com/blog/healing-the-body-with-frequencies-the-basics-explained, (accessed 14 October 2024).

[5] N. Biase, 'Sound Healing: What's Your Solfeggio Frequency?', *Spirituality & Health, A Unity Publication*, 2023, https://www.spiritualityhealth.com/sound-healing-whats-your-solfeggio-frequency, (accessed 14 October 2024).

[6] G. Markowsky, 'Information Theory', *Encyclopedia Britannica*, 2024, https://www.britannica.com/science/information-theory/Physiology, (accessed 14 October 2024).

[7] J. Wong and J. Brown, 'How Gratitude Changes You and Your Brain', *Mindful: Healthy Mind, Healthy Life*, 2017, https://www.mindful.org/gratitude-changes-brain, (accessed 14 October 2024).

[8] K. Cherry, 'What Is the Negativity Bias', *Very Well Mind*, 2023, https://www.verywellmind.com/negative-bias-4589618, (accessed 14 October 2024).

[9] M. Thorpe and R Ajmera, 'How Meditation Benefits Your Mind and Body', *Healthline*, 2024, https://www.healthline.com/nutrition/12-benefits-of-meditation, (accessed 14 October 2024).

[10] NHS, 'Mindfulness', *NHS*, 2022, https://www.nhs.uk/mental-health/self-help/tips-and-support/mindfulness, (accessed 14 October 2024).

[11] BDA: The Association of UK Dietitians, 'Mindful Eating', *BDA: The Association of UK Dieticians*, 2020, https://www.bda.uk.com/resource/mindful-eating.html, (accessed 14 October 2024).

[12] H. LeWine, 'The Power of the Placebo Effect', Massachusetts, *Harvard Health Publishing: Harvard Medical School*, 2024, https://www.health.harvard.edu/newsletter_article/the-power-of-the-placebo-effect, (accessed 14 October 2024).

[13] B. Busch, '9 Ways to Use Visualisation in Sport', *Inner Drive*, 2024, https://www.innerdrive.co.uk/blog/visualisation-in-sport, (accessed 14 October 2024).

[14] Mind.org, 'Nature and Mental Health', *Mind*, 2024, https://www.mind.org.uk/information-support/tips-for-everyday-living/nature-and-mental-health/how-nature-benefits-mental-health, (accessed 14 October 2024).

[15] Harvard Health Publishing: Harvard Medical School, 'A 20-minute Nature Break Relieves Stress', Massachusetts, *Harvard Health Publishing: Harvard Medical School*, 2024, https://www.health.harvard.edu/mind-and-mood/a-20-minute-nature-break-relieves-stress, (accessed 14 October 2024).

[16] A.W. Brooks et al., 'Don't Stop Believing: Rituals Improve Performance by Decreasing Anxiety', *Organizational Behavior and Human Design Processes*, no. 136, 2016, pp. 71-85, https://www.hbs.edu/ris/Publication%20Files/Rituals%20OBHDP_5cbc5848-ef4d-4192-a320-68d30169763c.pdf, (accessed 14 October 2024).

Printed in Great Britain
by Amazon